C. F. Adams.

Xmas – 1916.

PENROD AND SAM

"The obedient Verman marched into the closet and sat down among
the shoes and slippers, where he presented an interesting effect of
contrast"

PENROD AND SAM

BY
BOOTH TARKINGTON
AUTHOR OF "PENROD"

Illustrated by
WORTH BREHM

GARDEN CITY   NEW YORK
DOUBLEDAY, PAGE & COMPANY
1916

Copyright, 1916, by
DOUBLEDAY, PAGE & COMPANY

*All rights reserved, including that of
translation into foreign languages,
including the Scandinavian*

Copyright, 1914, 1915, 1916, by
INTERNATIONAL MAGAZINES CO. (COSMOPOLITAN MAGAZINE)

To
SUSANAH

CONTENTS

vii

CONTENTS

LIST OF ILLUSTRATIONS

PENROD AND SAM

CHAPTER I

D URING the daylight hours of several autumn Saturdays there had been severe outbreaks of cavalry in the Schofield neighbourhood. The sabres were of wood; the steeds were imaginary, and both were employed in a game called "bonded pris'ner" by its inventors, Masters Penrod Schofield and Samuel Williams. The pastime was not intricate. When two enemies met, they fenced spectacularly until the person of one or the other was touched by the opposing weapon; then, when the ensuing claims of foul play had been disallowed and the subsequent argument settled, the combatant touched was considered to be a prisoner until such time as he might be touched by the hilt of a sword belonging to one of his own party, which affected his release and restored to him the full enjoyment of hostile activity. Pending such rescue, however, he was obliged to accompany the forces of his captor whithersoever their strategical necessities led them, which included many

3

strange places. For the game was exciting, and, at
its highest pitch, would sweep out of an alley into a
stable, out of that stable and into a yard, out of that
yard and into a house, and through that house with
the sound (and effect upon furniture) of trampling
herds. In fact, this very similarity must have been
in the mind of the distressed coloured woman in Mrs.
Williams' kitchen, when she declared that she might
"jes' as well try to cook right spang in the middle o'
the stock-yards."

All up and down the neighbourhood the campaigns
were waged, accompanied by the martial clashing of
wood upon wood and by many clamorous arguments.

"You're a pris'ner, Roddy Bitts!"

"I am not!"

"You are, too! I touched you."

"Where, I'd like to know!"

"On the sleeve."

"You did not! I never felt it. I guess I'd 'a' felt
it, wouldn't I?"

"What if you didn't? I touched you, and you're
bonded. I leave it to Sam Williams."

"Yah! Course you would! He's on your side!
I leave it to Herman."

"No, you won't! If you can't show any *sense*

about it, we'll do it over, and I guess you'll *see*
whether you feel it or not! There! *Now*, I guess
you——"

"Aw, squash!"

Strangely enough, the undoubted champion proved
to be the youngest and darkest of all the combatants,
one Verman, coloured, brother to Herman, and sub-
stantially under the size to which his nine years entitled him. Verman was unfortunately tongue-tied,
but he was valiant beyond all others, and, in spite of
every handicap, he became at once the chief support
of his own party and the despair of the opposition.

On the third Saturday this opposition had been
worn down by the successive captures of Maurice
Levy and Georgie Bassett until it consisted of only
Sam Williams and Penrod. Hence, it behooved these
two to be wary, lest they be wiped out altogether; and
Sam was dismayed indeed, upon cautiously scouting
round a corner of his own stable, to find himself face
to face with the valorous and skilful Verman, who was
acting as an outpost, or picket, of the enemy.

Verman immediately fell upon Sam, horse and
foot, and Sam would have fled but dared not, for fear
he might be touched from the rear. Therefore, he de-
fended himself as best he could, and there followed a

lusty whacking, in the course of which Verman's hat, a relic and too large, fell from his head, touching Sam's weapon in falling.

"There!" panted Sam, desisting immediately. "That counts! You're bonded, Verman."

"Aim meewer!" Verman protested.

Interpreting this as, "Ain't neither," Sam invented a law to suit the occasion. "Yes, you are; that's the rule, Verman. I touched your hat with my sword, and your hat's just the same as you."

"Imm mop!" Verman insisted.

"Yes, it is," said Sam, already warmly convinced (by his own statement) that he was in the right. "Listen here! If I hit you on the shoe, it would be the same as hitting *you*, wouldn't it? I guess it'd count if I hit you on the shoe, wouldn't it? Well, a hat's just the same as shoes. Honest, that's the rule, Verman, and you're a pris'ner."

Now, in the arguing part of the game, Verman's impediment coöperated with a native amiability to render him far less effective than in the actual combat. He chuckled, and ceded the point.

"Aw wi," he said, and cheerfully followed his captor to a hidden place among some bushes in the front yard, where Penrod lurked.

"Looky what *I* got!" Sam said importantly, pushing his captive into this retreat. "*Now*, I guess you won't say I'm not so much use any more! Squat down, Verman, so's they can't see you if they're huntin' for us. That's one o' the rules—honest. You got to squat when we tell you to."

Verman was agreeable. He squatted, and then began to laugh uproariously.

"Stop that noise!" Penrod commanded. "You want to bekray us? What you laughin' at?"

"Ep mack im mimmup," Verman giggled.

"What's he mean?" asked Sam.

Penrod was more familiar with Verman's utterance, and he interpreted.

"He says they'll get him back in a minute."

"No, they won't. I'd just like to see——"

"Yes, they will, too," said Penrod. "They'll get him back for the main and simple reason we can't stay here all day, can we? And they'd find us anyhow, if we tried to. There's so many of 'em against just us two, they can run in and touch him soon as they get up to us—and then *he'll* be after us again and——"

"Listen here!" Sam interrupted. "Why can't we put some *real* bonds on him? We could put bonds on his wrists and around his legs—we could put 'em all over him, easy as nothin'. Then we could gag him——"

"No, we can't," said Penrod. "We can't, for the main and simple reason we haven't got any rope or anything to make the bonds with, have we? I wish we had some o' that stuff they give sick people. *Then,* I bet they wouldn't get him back so soon!"

"Sick people?" Sam repeated, not comprehending.

"It makes 'em go to sleep, no matter what you do to 'em," Penrod explained. "That's the main and simple reason they can't wake up, and you can cut off their ole legs—or their arms, or anything you want to."

"Hoy!" exclaimed Verman, in a serious tone. His laughter ceased instantly, and he began to utter a protest sufficiently intelligible.

"You needn't worry," Penrod said gloomily. "We haven't got any o' that stuff; so we can't do it."

"Well, we got to do sumpthing," said Sam.

His comrade agreed, and there was a thoughtful silence, but presently Penrod's countenance brightened.

"I know!" he exclaimed. "*I* know what we'll do with him. Why, I thought of it just as *easy* ! I can

most always think of things like that, for the main
and simple reason—well, I thought of it just as
soon——"

"Well, what is it?" Sam demanded crossly. Penrod's reiteration of his new-found phrase, "for the
main and simple reason," had been growing more and
more irksome to his friend all day, though Sam was
not definitely aware that the phrase was the cause of
his annoyance. "*What* are we goin' to do with him,
you know so much?"

Penrod rose and peered over the tops of the bushes,
shading his eyes with his hand, a gesture which was unnecessary but had a good appearance. He looked all
round about him in this manner, finally vouchsafing a
report to the impatient Sam.

"No enemies in sight—just for the main and simple
reason I expect they're all in the alley and in Georgie
Bassett's backyard."

"I bet they're not!" Sam said scornfully, his irritation much increased. "How do *you* know so much
about it?"

"Just for the main and simple reason," Penrod replied, with dignified finality.

And at that, Sam felt a powerful impulse to do
violence upon the person of his comrade-in-arms.

The emotion which prompted this impulse was so primitive and straightforward that it almost resulted in action, but Sam had a vague sense that he must control it as long as he could.

"Bugs!" he said.

Penrod was sensitive, and this cold word hurt him. However, he was under the domination of his strategic idea, and he subordinated private grievance to the common weal. ",Get up!" he commanded. "You get up, too, Verman. You got to—it's the rule. Now here—I'll *show* you what we're goin' to do. Stoop over, and both o' you do just exackly like *I* do. You watch *me*, because this biz'nuss has got to be done *right !*"

Sam muttered something; he was becoming more insurgent every moment, but he obeyed. Likewise, Verman rose to his feet, ducked his head between his shoulders, and trotted out to the sidewalk at Sam's heels, both following Penrod and assuming a stooping position in imitation of him. Verman was delighted with this phase of the game, and, also, he was profoundly amused by Penrod's pomposity. Something dim and deep within him perceived it to be cause for such merriment that he had ado to master himself, and was forced to bottle and cork his laughter with both hands. They proved insufficient; sputterings burst forth between his fingers.

"You stop that!" said Penrod, looking back darkly upon the prisoner.

Verman endeavoured to oblige, though giggles continued to leak from him at intervals, and the three boys stole along the fence in single file, proceeding in this fashion until they reached Penrod's own front gate. Here the leader ascertained, by a reconnaissance as far as the corner, that the hostile forces were still looking for them in another direction. He returned in a stealthy but important manner to his disgruntled follower and the hilarious captive.

"Well," said Sam impatiently, "I guess I'm not goin' to stand around here all day, I guess! You got anything you want to do, why'n't you go on and *do* it?"

Penrod's brow was already contorted to present the appearance of detached and lofty concentration—a histrionic failure, since it did not deceive the audience. He raised a hushing hand.

"*Sh!*" he murmured. "I got to think."

"Bugs!" said the impolite Mr. Williams again.

Verman bent double, squealing and sputtering; indeed, he was ultimately forced to sit upon the ground, so exhausting was the mirth to which he now gave way. Penrod's composure was somewhat affected, and he showed annoyance.

"Oh, I guess you won't laugh quite so much about a minute from now, ole Mister Verman!" he said severely. "You get up from there and do like I tell you."

"Well, why'n't you *tell* him why he won't laugh so much, then?" Sam demanded, as Verman rose. "Why'n't you do sumpthing and quit talkin' so much about it?"

Penrod haughtily led the way into the yard.

"You follow me," he said, "and I guess you'll learn a little sense!"

Then, abandoning his *hauteur* for an air of mystery equally irritating to Sam, he stole up the steps of the porch, and after a moment's manipulation of the knob of the big front door, contrived to operate the fastenings, and pushed the door open.

"Come on," he whispered, beckoning. And the three boys mounted the stairs to the floor above in silence—save for a belated giggle on the part of Verman, which was restrained upon a terrible gesture from Penrod. Verman buried his mouth as deeply as possible in a ragged sleeve, and confined his demonstrations to a heaving of the stomach and diaphragm.

Penrod led the way into the dainty room of his nineteen-year-old sister, Margaret, and closed the door.

"There," he said, in a low and husky voice, "I expect you'll see what I'm goin' to do now!"

"Well, what?" asked the skeptical Sam. "If we stay here very long your mother'll come and send us downstairs. What's the good of——"

"*Wait*, can't you?" Penrod wailed, in a whisper. "My goodness!" And going to an inner door, he threw it open, disclosing a clothes-closet hung with pretty garments of many kinds, while upon its floor were two rows of shoes and slippers of great variety and charm.

A significant thing is to be remarked concerning the door of this somewhat intimate treasury: there was no knob or latch upon the inner side, so that, when the door was closed, it could be opened only from the outside.

"There!" said Penrod. "You get in there, Verman, and I'll bet they won't get to touch you back out o' bein' our pris'ner very soon, *now!* Oh, I guess not!"

"Pshaw!" said Sam. "Is that all you were goin' to do? Why, your mother'll come and make him get out the first——"

"No, she won't. She and Margaret have gone to my aunt's in the country, and aren't goin' to be back till dark. And even if he made a lot o' noise, it's kind of hard to hear anything from in there, anyway, when the door's shut. Besides, he's got to keep quiet—that's the rule, Verman. You're a pris'ner, and it's the rule you can't holler or nothin'. You unnerstand that, Verman?"

"Aw wi," said Verman.

"Then go on in there. Hurry!"

The obedient Verman marched into the closet and sat down among the shoes and slippers, where he presented an interesting effect of contrast. He was still subject to hilarity—though endeavouring to suppress it by means of a patent-leather slipper—when Penrod closed the door.

"There!" said Penrod, leading the way from the room. "I guess *now* you see!"

Sam said nothing, and they came out to the open air, and reached their retreat in the Williams' yard again, without his having acknowledged Penrod's service to their mutual cause.

"I thought of that just as easy!" Penrod remarked, probably prompted to this odious bit of complacency by Sam's withholding the praise which might nat-

urally have been expected. And he was moved to
add, "I guess it'd of been a pretty long while if we'd
had to wait for you to think of sumpthing as good as
that, Sam."

"Why would it?" Sam asked. "Why would it of
been such a long while?"

"Oh," responded Penrod, airily, "just for the main
and simple reason!"

Sam could bear it no longer.

"Oh, hush up!" he shouted.

Penrod was stung.

"Do you mean *me*?" he demanded.

"Yes, I do!" replied the goaded Sam.

"Did you tell *me* to hush up?"

"Yes, I did!"

"I guess you don't know who you're talkin' to,"
Penrod said ominously. "I guess I just better show
you who you're talkin' to like that. I guess you need
a little sumpthing, for the main and simple——"

Sam uttered an uncontrollable howl and sprang
upon Penrod, catching him round the waist. Simultaneously with this impact, the wooden swords spun
through the air, and were presently trodden under-
foot as the two boys wrestled to and fro.

Penrod was not altogether surprised by the onset of

his friend. He had been aware of Sam's increasing irritation (though neither boy could have clearly stated its cause), and that very irritation produced a corresponding emotion in the bosom of the irritator. Mentally, Penrod was quite ready for the conflict— nay, he welcomed it—though, for the first few moments, Sam had the physical advantage.

However, it is proper that a neat distinction be drawn here. This was a conflict, but neither technically nor in the intention of the contestants was it a fight. Penrod and Sam were both in a state of high exasperation, and there was great bitterness; but no blows fell and no tears. They strained, they wrenched, they twisted, and they panted, and muttered: "Oh, no, you don't!" "Oh, I guess I do!" "Oh, you will, will you?" "You'll see what you get in about a minute!" "I guess you'll learn some sense this time!"

Streaks and blotches began to appear upon the two faces, where colour had been heightened by the ardent application of a cloth sleeve or shoulder, while ankles and insteps were scraped and toes were trampled. Turf and shrubberies suffered, also, as the struggle went on, until finally the wrestlers pitched headlong into a young lilac bush, and came to earth together, among its crushed and sprawling branches.

"*Ooch !*" and "*Wuf !*" were the two exclamations which marked this episode, and then, with no further comment, the struggle was energetically continued upon a horizontal plane. Now Penrod was on top, now Sam; they rolled, they squirmed, they suffered. And this contest endured. It went on and on, and it was impossible to imagine its coming to a definite termination. It went on so long that, to both the participants, it seemed to be a permanent thing, a condition which had always existed and which must always exist perpetually.

And thus they were discovered by a foray of the hostile party, headed by Roddy Bitts and Herman (older brother to Verman) and followed by the bonded prisoners, Maurice Levy and Georgie Bassett. These and others caught sight of the writhing figures, and charged down upon them with loud cries of triumph.

"Pris'ner! Pris'ner! Bonded pris'ner!" shrieked Roddy Bitts, and touched Penrod and Sam, each in turn, with his sabre. Then, seeing that they paid no attention and that they were at his mercy, he recalled the fact that several times, during earlier stages of the game, both of them had been unnecessarily vigorous in "touching" his own rather plump person. Therefore, the opportunity being excellent, he raised his weapon again, and, repeating the words "bonded pris'ner" as ample explanation of his deed, brought into play the full strength of his good right arm. He used the flat of the sabre.

Whack! Whack! Roddy was perfectly impartial. It was a cold-blooded performance and even more effective than he anticipated. For one thing, it ended the civil war instantly. Sam and Penrod leaped to their feet, shrieking and bloodthirsty, while Maurice Levy capered with joy, Herman was so overcome that he rolled upon the ground, and Georgie Bassett remarked virtuously:

"It serves them right for fighting."

But Roddy Bitts foresaw that something not within the rules of the game was about to happen.

"Here! You keep away from me!" he quavered, retreating. "I was just takin' you pris'ners. I guess I had a right to *touch* you, didn't I?"

Alas! Neither Sam nor Penrod was able to see the matter in that light. They had retrieved their own weapons, and they advanced upon Roddy, with a purposefulness that seemed horrible to him.

"Here! You keep away from me!" he said, in great alarm. "I'm goin' home."

He did go home—but only subsequently. What took place before his departure had the singular solidity and completeness of systematic violence; also, it bore the moral beauty of all actions which lead to peace and friendship, for, when it was over, and the final vocalizations of Roderick Magsworth Bitts, Junior, were growing faint with increasing distance, Sam and Penrod had forgotten their differences and felt well disposed toward each other once more. All their animosity was exhausted, and they were in a glow of good feeling, though probably they were not conscious of any direct gratitude to Roddy, whose thoughtful opportunism was really the cause of this happy result.

CHAPTER II

AFTER such rigorous events, every one comprehended that the game of bonded prisoner was over, and there was no suggestion that it should or might be resumed. The fashion of its conclusion had been so consummately enjoyed by all parties (with the natural exception of Roddy Bitts) that a renewal would have been tame; hence, the various minds of the company turned to other matters and became restless. Georgie Bassett withdrew first, remembering that if he expected to be as wonderful as usual, to-morrow, in Sunday-school, it was time to prepare himself, though this was not included in the statement he made alleging the cause of his departure. Being detained bodily and pressed for explanation, he desperately said that he had to go home to tease the cook—which had the rakehelly air he thought would insure his release, but was not considered plausible. However, he was finally allowed to go, and, as first hints of evening

20

were already cooling and darkening the air, the party broke up, its members setting forth, whistling, toward their several homes, though Penrod lingered with Sam. Herman was the last to go from them.

"Well, I got git 'at stove-wood f' suppuh," he said, rising and stretching himself. "I got git 'at lil' soap-box wagon, an' go on ovuh wheres 'at new house buil'in' on Secon' Street; pick up few shingles an' blocks layin' roun'."

He went through the yard toward the alley, and, at the alley gate, remembering something, he paused and called to them. The lot was a deep one, and they were too far away to catch his meaning. Sam shouted, "Can't *hear* you," and Herman replied, but still unintelligibly; then, upon Sam's repetition of "Can't *hear* you," Herman waved his arm in farewell, implying that the matter was of little significance, and vanished. But if they had understood him, Penrod and Sam might have considered his inquiry of instant importance, for Herman's last shout was to ask if either of them had noticed "where Verman went."

Verman and Verman's whereabouts were, at this hour, of no more concern to Sam and Penrod than was the other side of the moon. That unfortunate bonded prisoner had been long since utterly effaced from their fields of consciousness, and the dark secret of their Bastille troubled them not—for the main and simple reason that they had forgotten it.

They drifted indoors, and found Sam's mother's white cat drowsing on a desk in the library, the which coincidence obviously inspired the experiment of ascertaining how successfully ink could be used in making a clean white cat look like a coach-dog. There was neither malice nor mischief in their idea; simply, a problem presented itself to the biological and artistic questionings beginning to stir within them. They did not mean to do the cat the slightest injury or to cause her any pain. They were above teasing cats, and they merely detained this one and made her feel a little wet—at considerable cost to themselves from both the ink and the cat. However, at the conclusion of their efforts, it was thought safer to drop the cat out of the window before anybody came, and, after some hasty work with blotters, the desk was moved to cover certain sections of the rug, and the two boys repaired to the bathroom for hot water and soap. They knew they had done nothing wrong, but they felt easier when the only traces remaining upon them were the less prominent ones upon their garments.

These precautions taken, it was time for them to make their appearance at Penrod's house for dinner, for it had been arranged, upon petition, earlier in the day, that Sam should be his friend's guest for the evening meal. Clean to the elbows and with light hearts, they set forth. They marched, whistling—though not producing a distinctly musical effect, since neither had any particular air in mind —and they found nothing wrong with the world; they had not a care. Arrived at their adjacent destination, they found Miss Margaret Schofield just entering the front door.

"Hurry, boys!" she said. "Mamma came home long before I did, and I'm sure dinner is waiting. Run on out to the dining-room and tell them I'll be right down."

And, as they obeyed, she mounted the stairs, humming a little tune and unfastening the clasp of the long, light-blue military cape she wore. She went to her own quiet room, lit the gas, removed her hat, and placed it and the cape upon the bed; after which she gave her hair a push, subsequent to her scrutiny of a mirror; then, turning out the light, she went as far as the door. Being an orderly girl, she returned to the bed and took the cape and the hat to her clothes-closet. She opened the door of this sanctuary, and, in the dark, hung her cape upon a hook and placed her hat upon the shelf. Then she closed the door again, having noted nothing unusual, though she had an impression that the place needed airing. She descended to the dinner table.

The other members of the family were already occupied with the meal, and the visitor was replying politely, in his non-masticatory intervals, to inquiries concerning the health of his relatives. So sweet and assured was the condition of Sam and Penrod, that Margaret's arrival from her room meant nothing to them. Their memories were not stirred, and they continued eating, their expressions brightly placid.

But from out of doors there came the sound of a calling and questing voice, at first in the distance, then growing louder—coming nearer.

"Oh, Ver-er-man! O-o-o-oh, Ver-er-ma-a-an!"

It was the voice of Herman.

"*Oo-o-o-o-oh, Ver-er-er-ma-a-a-an!*"

And then two boys sat stricken at that cheerful table and ceased to eat. Recollection awoke with a bang!

"Oh, my!" Sam gasped.

"What's the matter?" said Mr. Schofield. "Swallow something the wrong way, Sam?"

"Ye-es, sir."

"*Oo-o-o-oh, Ver-er-er-ma-a-an !*"

And now the voice was near the windows of the dining-room.

Penrod, very pale, pushed back his chair and jumped up.

"What's the matter with *you?*" his father demanded. "Sit down!"

"It's Herman—that coloured boy lives in the alley," said Penrod hoarsely. "I—expect—I think——"

"Well, what's the matter?"

"I think his little brother's maybe got lost, and Sam and I better go help look——"

"You'll do nothing of the kind," said Mr. Schofield sharply. "Sit down and eat your dinner."

In a palsy, the miserable boy resumed his seat. He and Sam exchanged a single dumb glance; then the eyes of both swung fearfully to Margaret. Her appearance was one of sprightly content, and, from a certain point of view, nothing could have been more alarming. If she had opened her closet door without discovering Verman, that must have been because Verman was dead and Margaret had failed to notice the body. (Such were the thoughts of Penrod and Sam.) But she might not have opened the closet door. And whether she had or not, Verman must still be there, alive or dead, for if he had escaped he would have gone home, and their ears would not be ringing with the sinister and melancholy cry that now came from the distance, "*Oo-o-oh, Ver-er-ma-an!*"

Verman, in his seclusion, did not hear that appeal from his brother; there were too many walls between them. But he was becoming impatient for release, though, all in all, he had not found the confinement intolerable or even very irksome. His character was philosophic, his imagination calm; no bugaboos came to trouble him. When the boys closed the door upon him, he made himself comfortable upon the floor and, for a time, thoughtfully chewed a patent-leather slipper that had come under his hand. He found the patent leather not unpleasant to his palate, though he swallowed only a portion of what he detached, not being hungry at that time. The soul-fabric of Verman was of a fortunate weave; he was not a seeker and questioner. When it happened to him that he was at rest in a shady corner, he did not even think about a place in the sun. Verman took life as it came.

Naturally, he fell asleep. And toward the conclusion of his slumbers, he had this singular adventure: a lady set her foot down within less than half an inch of his nose—and neither of them knew it. Verman slept on, without being wakened by either the closing or the opening of the door. What did rouse him was something ample and soft falling upon him—Margaret's cape, which slid from the hook after she had gone.

Enveloped in its folds, Verman sat up, corkscrewing his knuckles into the corners of his eyes. Slowly he became aware of two important vacuums—one in time and one in his stomach. Hours had vanished strangely into nowhere; the game of bonded prisoner was something cloudy and remote of the long, long ago, and, although Verman knew where he was, he had partially forgotten how he came there. He perceived, however, that something had gone wrong, for he was certain that he ought not to be where he found himself.

White-Folks' House! The fact that Verman could not have pronounced these words rendered them no less clear in his mind; they began to stir his apprehension, and nothing becomes more rapidly tumultuous than apprehension once it is stirred. That he might possibly obtain release by making a noise was too daring a thought and not even conceived, much less entertained, by the little and humble Verman. For, with the bewildering gap of his slumber between him and previous events, he did not place the responsibility for his being in White-Folks' House upon the white folks who had put him there. His state of mind was that of the stable-puppy who knows he *must* not be found in the parlour. Not thrice in his life had Verman been within the doors of White-Folks' House, and, above all things, he felt that it was in some undefined way vital to him to get out of White-Folks' House unobserved and unknown. It was in his very blood to be sure of that.

Further than this point, the processes of Verman's mind become mysterious to the observer. It appears, however, that he had a definite (though somewhat primitive) conception of the usefulness of disguise; and he must have begun his preparations before he heard footsteps in the room outside his closed door.

These footsteps were Margaret's. Just as Mr. Schofield's coffee was brought, and just after Penrod had been baffled in another attempt to leave the table, Margaret rose and patted her father impertinently upon the head.

"You can't bully *me* that way!" she said. "I got home too late to dress, and I'm going to a dance. 'Scuse!"

And she began her dancing on the spot, pirouetting herself swiftly out of the room, and was immediately heard running up the stairs.

"Penrod!" Mr. Schofield shouted. "Sit down! How many times am I going to tell you? What *is* the matter with you to-night?"

"I *got* to go," gasped Penrod. "I got to tell Margaret sumpthing."

"What have you 'got' to tell her?"

"It's—it's sumpthing I forgot to tell her."

"Well, it will keep till she comes downstairs," said Mr. Schofield grimly. "You sit down till this meal is finished."

Penrod was becoming frantic.

"I got to tell her—it's sumpthing Sam's mother told me to tell her," he babbled. "Didn't she, Sam? You heard her tell me to tell her; didn't you, Sam?"

. Sam offered prompt corroboration.

"Yes, sir; she did. She said for us both to tell her. I better go, too, I guess, because she said——"

He was interrupted. Startlingly upon their ears rang shriek on shriek. Mrs. Schofield, recognizing Margaret's voice, likewise shrieked, and Mr. Schofield uttered various sounds, but Penrod and Sam were incapable of doing anything vocally. All rushed from the table.

Margaret continued to shriek, and it is not to be denied that there was some cause for her agitation. When she opened the closet door, her light-blue military cape, instead of hanging on the hook where she had left it, came out into the room in a manner which she afterward described as "a kind of horrible creep, but faster than a creep." Nothing was to be seen except the creeping cape, she said, but, of course, she could tell there was some awful thing inside of it. It was too large to be a cat, and too small to be a boy; it was too large to be Duke, Penrod's little old dog, and, besides, Duke wouldn't act like that. It crept rapidly out into the upper hall, and then, as she recovered the use of her voice and began to scream, the animated cape abandoned its creeping for a quicker gait—"a weird, heaving flop," she defined it.

The Thing then decided upon a third style of locomotion, evidently, for when Sam and Penrod reached the front hall, a few steps in advance of Mr. and Mrs. Schofield, it was rolling grandly down the stairs.

Mr. Schofield had only a hurried glimpse of it as it reached the bottom, close by the front door.

"Grab that thing!" he shouted, dashing forward. "Stop it! Hit it!"

It was at this moment that Sam Williams displayed the presence of mind which was his most eminent characteristic. Sam's wonderful instinct for the right action almost never failed him in a crisis, and it did not fail him now. Leaping to the door, at the very instant when the rolling cape touched it, Sam flung the door open—and the cape rolled on. With incredible rapidity and intelligence, it rolled, indeed, out into the night.

Penrod jumped after it, and the next second reappeared in the doorway holding the cape. He shook out its folds, breathing hard but acquiring confidence. In fact, he was able to look up in his father's face and say, with bright ingenuousness

"It was just laying there. Do you know what I think? Well, it couldn't have acted that way itself.

I think there must have been sumpthing kind of inside of it!"

Mr. Schofield shook his head slowly, in marvelling admiration.

"Brilliant—oh, brilliant!" he murmured, while Mrs. Schofield ran to support the enfeebled form of Margaret at the top of the stairs.

. . . In the library, after Margaret's departure to her dance, Mr. and Mrs. Schofield were still discussing the visitation, Penrod having accompanied his homeward-bound guest as far as the front gate.

"No; you're wrong," said Mrs. Schofield, upholding a theory, earlier developed by Margaret, that the animated behaviour of the cape could be satisfactorily explained on no other ground than the supernatural. "You see, the boys saying they couldn't remember what Mrs. Williams wanted them to tell Margaret, and that probably she hadn't told them anything to tell her, because most likely they'd misunderstood something she said—well, of course, all that does sound mixed-up and peculiar, but they sound that way about half the time, anyhow. No; it couldn't possibly have had a thing to do with it. They were right there at the table with us all the time, and they came straight to the table the minute they entered the house. Before that, they'd been over at Sam's all afternoon. So, it *couldn't* have been the boys." Mrs. Schofield paused to ruminate with a little air of pride, then added: "Margaret has often thought—oh, long before this! —that she was a medium. I mean—if she would let herself. So it wasn't anything the boys did."

Mr. Schofield grunted.

"I'll admit this much," he said. "I'll admit it wasn't anything we'll ever get out of 'em."

And the remarks of Sam and Penrod, taking leave of each other, one on each side of the gate, appeared to corroborate Mr. Schofield's opinion.

"Well, g'-night, Penrod," Sam said. "It was a pretty good Saturday, wasn't it?"

"Fine!" said Penrod casually. "G'-night, Sam."

CHAPTER III

THE MILITARIST

PENROD SCHOFIELD, having been "kept in" for the unjust period of twenty minutes after school, emerged to a deserted street. That is, the street was deserted so far as Penrod was concerned. Here and there people were to be seen upon the sidewalks, but they were adults, and they and the shade trees had about the same quality of significance in Penrod's consciousness. Usually he saw grown people in the mass, which is to say, they were virtually invisible to him, though exceptions must be taken in favour of policemen, firemen, street-car conductors, motormen, and all other men in any sort of uniform or regalia. But this afternoon none of these met the roving eye, and Penrod set out upon his homeward way wholly dependent upon his own resources.

To one of Penrod's inner texture, a mere unadorned walk from one point to another was intolerable, and he had not gone a block without achieving some slight remedy for the tameness of life. An electric-light pole at the corner, invested with powers of observation, might have been surprised to find itself suddenly enacting a rôle of dubious honour in improvised melodrama. Penrod, approaching, gave the pole a look of sharp suspicion, then one of conviction; slapped it lightly and contemptuously with his open hand; passed on a few paces, but turned abruptly, and, pointing his right forefinger, uttered the symbolic word, "Bing!"

The plot was somewhat indefinite; yet nothing is more certain than that the electric-light pole had first attempted something against him, then growing bitter when slapped, and stealing after him to take him treacherously in the back, had got itself shot through and through by one too old in such warfare to be caught off his guard.

Leaving the body to lie where it was, he placed the smoking pistol in a holster at his saddlebow—he had decided that he was mounted—and proceeded up the street. At intervals he indulged himself in other encounters, reining in at first suspicion of ambush with a muttered, "Whoa, Charlie!" or "Whoa, Mike!" or even "Whoa, Washington!" for preoccupation with the enemy outweighed at-

Bingy Bing went the other and two more went meet their Maker!

36 PENROD AND SAM

tention to the details of theatrical consistency,
though the steed's varying names were at least har-
moniously masculine, since a boy, in these creative
moments, never rides a mare. And having brought
Charlie or Mike or Washington to a standstill,
Penrod would draw the sure weapon from its holster
and—"Bing! Bing! Bing!"—let them have it.

It is not to be understood that this was a noisy
performance, or even an obvious one. It attracted
no attention from any pedestrian, and it was to be
perceived only that a boy was proceeding up the
street at a somewhat irregular gait. Three or four
years earlier, when Penrod was seven or eight, he
would have shouted "Bing!" at the top of his voice;
he would have galloped openly; all the world might
have seen that he bestrode a charger. But a change
had come upon him with advancing years. Although the grown people in sight were indeed to
him as walking trees, his dramas were accomplished
principally by suggestion and symbol. His "Whoas"
and "Bings" were delivered in a husky whisper, and
his equestrianism was established by action mostly
of the mind, the accompanying artistry of the feet
being unintelligible to the passerby.

And yet, though he concealed from observation

the stirring little scenes he thus enacted, a love of realism was increasing within him. Early childhood is not fastidious about the accessories of its drama— a cane is vividly a gun which may instantly, as vividly, become a horse; but at Penrod's time of life the lath sword is no longer satisfactory. Indeed, he now had a vague sense that weapons of wood were unworthy to the point of being contemptible and ridiculous, and he employed them only when he was alone and unseen. For months a yearning had grown more and more poignant in his vitals, and this yearning was symbolized by one of his most profound secrets. In the inner pocket of his jacket he carried a bit of wood whittled into the distant likeness of a pistol, but not even Sam Williams had seen it. The wooden pistol never knew the light of day, save when Penrod was in solitude; and yet it never left his side except at night, when it was placed under his pillow. Still, it did not satisfy; it was but the token of his yearning and his dream. With all his might and main Penrod longed for one thing beyond all others. He wanted a Real Pistol!

That was natural. Pictures of real pistols being used to magnificently romantic effect were upon almost all the billboards in town, the year round;

and as for the "movie" shows, they could not have
lived an hour unpistoled. In the drug store, where
Penrod bought his candy and soda when he was in
funds, he would linger to turn the pages of periodicals
whose illustrations were fascinatingly pistolic. Some
of the magazines upon the very library table at
home were sprinkled with pictures of people (usually
in evening clothes) pointing pistols at other people.
Nay, the Library Board of the town had emitted a
"Selected List of Fifteen Books for Boys," and
Penrod had read fourteen of them with pleasure,
but as the fifteenth contained no weapons in the
earlier chapters and held forth little prospect of any
shooting at all, he abandoned it halfway, and read
the most sanguinary of the other fourteen over
again. So, the daily food of his imagination being
gun, what wonder that he thirsted for the Real!

He passed from the sidewalk into his own yard,
with a subdued "Bing!" inflicted upon the stolid
person of a gatepost, and, entering the house through
the kitchen, ceased to bing for a time. However,
driven back from the fore part of the house by a
dismal sound of callers, he returned to the kitchen
and sat down.

"Della," he said to the cook, "do you know what

I'd do if you was a crook and I had my ottomatic
with me?"

Della was industrious and preoccupied. "If I was
a cook!" she repeated ignorantly, and with no cordiality. "Well, I *am* a cook. I'm a-cookin' right
now. Either g'wan in the house where y'b'long, or
git out in th' yard!"

Penrod chose the latter, and betook himself slowly
to the back fence, where he was greeted in a boisterous manner by his wistful little old dog, Duke, returning from some affair of his own in the alley.

"Get down!" said Penrod coldly, and bestowed a
spiritless "Bing!" upon him.

At this moment a shout was heard from the alley,
"Yay, Penrod!" and the sandy head of comrade
Sam Williams appeared above the fence.

"Come on over," said Penrod.

As Sam obediently climbed the fence, the little
old dog, Duke, moved slowly away, but presently,
glancing back over his shoulder and seeing the two
boys standing together, he broke into a trot and
disappeared round a corner of the house. He was
a dog of long and enlightening experience; and he
made it clear that the conjunction of Penrod and
Sam portended events which, from his point of view,

might be unfortunate. Duke had a forgiving disposition, but he also possessed a melancholy wisdom. In the company of either Penrod or Sam, alone, affection often caused him to linger, albeit with a little pessimism, but when he saw them together, he invariably withdrew in as unobtrusive a manner as haste would allow.

"What you doin'?" Sam asked.

"Nothin'. What you?"

"I'll show you if you'll come over to our house," said Sam, who was wearing an important and secretive expression.

"What for?" Penrod showed little interest.

"Well, I said I'd show you if you came on over, didn't I?"

"But you haven't got anything I haven't got," said Penrod indifferently. "I know everything that's in your yard and in your stable, and there isn't a thing——"

"I didn't say it was in the yard or in the stable, did I?"

"Well, there ain't anything in your house," returned Penrod frankly, "that I'd walk two feet to look at—not a thing!"

"Oh, no!" Sam assumed mockery. "Oh, no,

you wouldn't! You know what it is, don't you?
Yes, you do!"

Penrod's curiosity stirred somewhat.

"Well, all right," he said, "I got nothin' to do.
I just as soon go. What is it?"

"You wait and see," said Sam, as they climbed
the fence. "I bet *your* ole eyes'll open pretty far
in about a minute or so!"

"I bet they don't. It takes a good deal to get me
excited, unless it's sumpthing mighty——"

"You'll see!" Sam promised.

He opened an alley gate and stepped into his own
yard in a manner signalling caution—though the
exploit, thus far, certainly required none—and Penrod began to be impressed and hopeful. They
entered the house, silently, encountering no one,
and Sam led the way upstairs, tiptoeing, implying
unusual and increasing peril. Turning, in the upper
hall, they went into Sam's father's bedroom, and
Sam closed the door with a caution so genuine that
already Penrod's eyes began to fulfil his host's prediction. Adventures in another boy's house are
trying to the nerves; and another boy's father's
bedroom, when invaded, has a violated sanctity
that is almost appalling. Penrod felt that some-

thing was about to happen—something much more important than he had anticipated.

Sam tiptoed across the room to a chest of drawers, and, kneeling, carefully pulled out the lowest drawer until the surface of its contents—Mr. Williams' winter underwear—lay exposed. Then he fumbled beneath the garments and drew forth a large object, displaying it triumphantly to the satisfactorily dumfounded Penrod.

It was a blue-steel Colt's revolver, of the heaviest pattern made in the Seventies. Mr. Williams had inherited it from Sam's grandfather (a small man, a deacon, and dyspeptic) and it was larger and more horrible than any revolver either of the boys had ever seen in any picture, moving or stationary. Moreover, greenish bullets of great size were to be seen in the chambers of the cylinder, suggesting massacre rather than mere murder. This revolver was Real and it was Loaded!

CHAPTER IV

BINGISM

BOTH boys lived breathlessly through a magnificent moment.

"Leave me have it!" gasped Penrod. "Leave me have hold of it!"

"You wait a minute!" Sam protested, in a whisper. "I want to show you how I do."

"No; you let me show you how *I* do!" Penrod insisted; and they scuffled for possession.

"Look out!" Sam whispered warningly. "It might go off."

"Then you better leave me have it!" And Penrod, victorious and flushed, stepped back, the weapon in his grasp. "Here," he said, "this is the way I do: You be a crook; and suppose you got a dagger, and I——"

"I don't want any dagger," Sam protested, advancing. "I want that revolaver. It's my father's revolaver, ain't it?"

"Well, *wait* a minute, can't you? I got a right to

show you the way I *do*, first, haven't I?" Penrod
began an improvisation on the spot. "Say I'm
comin' along after dark like this—look, Sam! And
say you try to make a jump at me——"

"I won't!" Sam declined this rôle impatiently.
"I guess it ain't *your* father's revolaver, is it?"

"Well, it may be your father's but it ain't yours,"
Penrod argued, becoming logical. "It ain't either's
of us revolaver, so I got as much right——"

"You haven't either. It's my fath——"

"*Watch*, can't you—just a minute!" Penrod urged
vehemently. "I'm not goin' to keep it, am I?
You can have it when I get through, can't you?
Here's how *I* do: I'm comin' along after dark, just
walkin' along this way—like this—look, Sam!"

Penrod, suiting the action to the word, walked to
the other end of the room, swinging the revolver at
his side with affected carelessness.

"I'm just walkin' along like this, and first I don't
see you," continued the actor. "Then I kind of
get a notion sumpthing wrong's liable to happen,
so I—— No!" He interrupted himself abruptly.
"No; that isn't it. You wouldn't notice that I
had my good ole revolaver with me. You wouldn't
think I had one, because it'd be under my coat like

this, and you wouldn't see it." Penrod stuck the muzzle of the pistol into the waistband of his knickerbockers at the left side and, buttoning his jacket, sustained the weapon in concealment by pressure of his elbow. "So you think I haven't got any; you think I'm just a man comin' along, and so you——"

Sam advanced. "Well, you've had your turn," he said. "Now, it's mine. I'm goin' to show you how I——"

"*Watch* me, can't you?" Penrod wailed. "I haven't showed you how *I* do, have I? My goodness! Can't you watch me a minute?"

"I *have* been! You said yourself it'd be my turn soon as you——"

"My goodness! Let me have a *chance*, can't you?" Penrod retreated to the wall, turning his right side toward Sam and keeping the revolver still protected under his coat. "I got to have my turn first, haven't I?"

"Well, yours is over long ago."

"It isn't either! I——"

"Anyway," said Sam decidedly, clutching him by the right shoulder and endeavouring to reach his left side—"anyway, I'm goin' to have it now."

"You said I could have my turn out!" Penrod, carried away by indignation, raised his voice.

"I did not!" Sam, likewise lost to caution, asserted his denial loudly.

"You did, too."

"You said——"

"I never said anything!"

"You said—— Quit that!"

"Boys!" Mrs. Williams, Sam's mother, opened the door of the room and stood upon the threshold. The scuffling of Sam and Penrod ceased instantly, and they stood hushed and stricken, while fear fell upon them. "Boys, you weren't quarrelling, were you?"

"Ma'am?" said Sam.

"Were you quarrelling with Penrod?"

"No, ma'am," answered Sam in a small voice.

"It sounded like it. What was the matter?"

Both boys returned her curious glance with meekness. They were summoning their faculties—which were needed. Indeed, these are the crises which prepare a boy for the business difficulties of his later life. Penrod, with the huge weapon beneath his jacket, insecurely supported by an elbow and by a waistband which he instantly began to

distrust, experienced distressful sensations similar
to those of the owner of too heavily insured
property carrying a gasoline can under his overcoat
and detained for conversation by a policeman. And
if, in the coming years, it was to be Penrod's lot to
find himself in that precise situation, no doubt he
would be the better prepared for it on account of
this present afternoon's experience under the scald-
ing eye of Mrs. Williams. It should be added that
Mrs. Williams's eye was awful to the imagination
only. It was a gentle eye and but mildly curious,
having no remote suspicion of the dreadful truth,
for Sam had backed upon the chest of drawers and
closed the damnatory open one with the calves of his
legs.

Sam, not bearing the fatal evidence upon his
person, was in a better state than Penrod, though
when boys fall into the stillness now assumed by
these two, it should be understood that they are
suffering. Penrod, in fact, was the prey to apprehension so keen that the actual pit of his stomach
was cold.

Being the actual custodian of the crime, he understood that his case was several degrees more serious
than that of Sam, who, in the event of detection,

would be convicted as only an accessory. It was a
lesson, and Penrod already repented his selfishness in
not allowing Sam to show how he did, first.

"You're sure you weren't quarrelling, Sam?" said
Mrs. Williams.

"No, ma'am; we were just talking.'

Still she seemed dimly uneasy, and her eye swung
to Penrod.

"What were you and Sam talking about, Penrod?"

"Ma'am?"

"What were you talking about?"

Penrod gulped invisibly.

"Well," he murmured, "it wasn't much. Different things."

"What things?"

"Oh, just sumpthing. Different things."

"I'm glad you weren't quarrelling," said Mrs.
Williams, reassured by this reply, which, though
somewhat baffling, was thoroughly familiar to her
ear. "Now, if you'll come downstairs, I'll give you
each one cookie and no more, so your appetites
won't be spoiled for your dinners."

She stood, evidently expecting them to precede
her. To linger might renew vague suspicion, causing it to become more definite; and boys preserve

themselves from moment to moment, not often attempting to secure the future. Consequently, the apprehensive Sam and the unfortunate Penrod (with the monstrous implement bulking against his ribs) walked out of the room and down the stairs, their countenances indicating an interior condition of solemnity. And a curious shade of behaviour might have here interested a criminologist. Penrod endeavoured to keep as close to Sam as possible, like a lonely person seeking company, while, on the other hand, Sam kept moving away from Penrod, seeming to desire an appearance of aloofness.

"Go into the library, boys," said Mrs. Williams, as the three reached the foot of the stairs. "I'll bring you your cookies. Papa's in there."

Under her eye the two entered the library, to find Mr. Williams reading his evening paper. He looked up pleasantly, but it seemed to Penrod that he had an ominous and penetrating expression.

"What have you been up to, you boys?" inquired this enemy.

"Nothing," said Sam. "Different things."

"What like?"

"Oh—just different things."

Mr. Williams nodded; then his glance rested casually upon Penrod.

"What's the matter with your arm, Penrod?"

Penrod became paler, and Sam withdrew from him almost conspicuously.

"Sir?"

"I said, What's the matter with your arm?"

"Which one?" Penrod quavered.

"Your left. You seem to be holding it in an unnatural position. Have you hurt it?"

Penrod swallowed. "Yes, sir. A boy bit me—I mean a dog—a dog bit me."

Mr. Williams murmured sympathetically: "That's too bad! Where did he bite you?"

"On the—right on the elbow."

"Good gracious! Perhaps you ought to have it cauterized."

"Sir?"

"Did you have a doctor look at it?"

"No, sir. My mother put some stuff from the drug store on it."

"Oh, I see. Probably it's all right, then."

"Yes, sir." Penrod drew breath more freely, and accepted the warm cookie Mrs. Williams brought him. He ate it without relish.

"You can have only one apiece," she said. "It's too near dinner-time. You needn't beg for any more, because you can't have 'em."

They were good about that; they were in no frame of digestion for cookies.

"Was it your own dog that bit you?" Mr. Williams inquired.

"Sir? No, sir. It wasn't Duke."

"Penrod!" Mrs. Williams exclaimed. "When did it happen?"

"I don't remember just when," he answered feebly. "I guess it was day before yesterday."

"Gracious! How did it——"

"He—he just came up and bit me."

"Why, that's terrible! It might be dangerous for other children," said Mrs. Williams, with a solicitous glance at Sam. "Don't you know whom he belongs to?"

"No'm. It was just a dog."

"You poor boy! Your mother must have been dreadfully frightened when you came home and she saw——"

She was interrupted by the entrance of a middle-aged coloured woman. "Miz Williams," she began, and then, as she caught sight of Penrod, she addressed him directly, "You' ma telefoam if you here, send you home right away, 'cause they waitin' dinner on you."

"Run along, then," said Mrs. Williams, patting the visitor lightly upon his shoulder; and she accompanied him to the front door. "Tell your mother I'm so sorry about your getting bitten, and you must take good care of it, Penrod."

"Yes'm."

Penrod lingered helplessly outside the doorway, looking at Sam, who stood partially obscured in the hall, behind Mrs. Williams. Penrod's eyes, with a veiled anguish, conveyed a pleading for help as well as a horror of the position in which he found himself. Sam, however, pale and determined, seemed to have assumed a stony attitude of detachment, as if it were well understood between them that his own comparative innocence was established, and that whatever catastrophe ensued, Penrod had brought it on and must bear the brunt of it alone.

"Well, you'd better run along, since they're waiting for you at home," said Mrs. Williams, closing the door. "Good-night, Penrod."

. . . Ten minutes later Penrod took his place

at his own dinner-table, somewhat breathless but with an expression of perfect composure.

"Can't you *ever* come home without being telephoned for?" demanded his father.

"Yes, sir." And Penrod added reproachfully, placing the blame upon members of Mr. Schofield's own class, "Sam's mother and father kept me, or I'd been home long ago. They would keep on talkin', and I guess I had to be *polite*, didn't I?"

His left arm was as free as his right; there was no dreadful bulk beneath his jacket, and at Penrod's age the future is too far away to be worried about. The difference between temporary security and permanent security is left for grown people. To Penrod, security was security, and before his dinner was half eaten his spirit had become fairly serene.

Nevertheless, when he entered the empty carriage-house of the stable, on his return from school the next afternoon, his expression was not altogether without apprehension, and he stood in the doorway looking well about him before he lifted a loosened plank in the flooring and took from beneath it the grand old weapon of the Williams family. Nor did his eye lighten with any pleasurable excitement as he sat himself down in a shadowy corner and

began some sketchy experiments with the mechanism. The allure of first sight was gone. In
Mr. Williams' bedchamber, with Sam clamouring
for possession, it had seemed to Penrod that nothing
in the world was so desirable as to have that revolver
in his own hands—it was his dream come true.
But, for reasons not definitely known to him, the
charm had departed; he turned the cylinder gingerly,
almost with distaste; and slowly there stole over
him a feeling that there was something repellent
and threatening in the heavy blue steel.

Thus does the long-dreamed Real misbehave—
not only for Penrod!

More out of a sense of duty to bingism in general
than for any other reason, he pointed the revolver
at the lawn-mower, and gloomily murmured, "Bing!"

Simultaneously, a low and cautious voice sounded
from the yard outside, "Yay, Penrod!" and Sam
Williams darkened the doorway, his eye falling instantly upon the weapon in his friend's hand. Sam
seemed relieved to see it.

"You didn't get caught with it, did you?" he
said hastily.

Penrod shook his head, rising.

"I guess not! I guess I got *some* brains around

me," he added, inspired by Sam's presence to assume a slight swagger. "They'd have to get up pretty early to find any good ole revolaver, once I got *my* hands on it!"

"I guess we can keep it, all right," Sam said confidentially. "Because this morning papa was putting on his winter underclothes and he found it wasn't there, and they looked all over and everywhere, and he was pretty mad, and said he knew it was those cheap plumbers stole it that mamma got instead of the regular plumbers he always used to have, and he said there wasn't any chance ever gettin' it back, because you couldn't tell which one took it, and they'd all swear it wasn't them. So it looks like we could keep it for our revolaver, Penrod, don't it? I'll give you half of it."

Penrod affected some enthusiasm. "Sam, we'll keep it out here in the stable."

"Yes, and we'll go huntin' with it. We'll do lots of things with it!" But Sam made no effort to take it, and neither boy seemed to feel yesterday's necessity to show the other how he did. "Wait till next Fourth o' July!" Sam continued. "Oh, oh! Look out!"

This incited a genuine spark from Penrod.

"Fourth o' July! I guess she'll be a little better than any firecrackers! Just a little 'Bing! Bing! Bing!' she'll be goin'. 'Bing! Bing! Bing!'"

The suggestion of noise stirred his comrade. "I'll bet she'll go off louder'n that time the gas-works blew up! I wouldn't be afraid to shoot her off *any* time."

"I bet you would," said Penrod. "You aren't used to revolavers the way I——"

"You aren't, either!" Sam exclaimed promptly. "I wouldn't be any more afraid to shoot her off than you would."

"You would, too!"

"I would not!"

"Well, let's see you then; you talk so much!" And Penrod handed the weapon scornfully to Sam, who at once became less self-assertive.

"I'd shoot her off in a minute," Sam said, "only it might break sumpthing if it hit it."

"Hold her up in the air, then. It can't hurt the roof, can it?"

Sam, with a desperate expression, lifted the revolver at arm's length. Both boys turned away their heads, and Penrod put his fingers in his ears—but nothing happened. "What's the matter?" he

demanded. "Why don't you go on if you're goin'
to?"

Sam lowered his arm. "I guess I didn't have her
cocked," he said apologetically, whereupon Penrod
loudly jeered.

"Tryin' to shoot a revolaver and didn't know
enough to cock her! If I didn't know any more
about revolavers than that, I'd——"

"There!" Sam exclaimed, managing to draw back
the hammer until two chilling clicks warranted his
opinion that the pistol was now ready to perform
its office. "I guess she'll do all right to suit you *this*
time!"

"Well, why'n't you go ahead, then; you know so
much!" And as Sam raised his arm, Penrod again
turned away his head and placed his forefingers in
his ears.

A pause followed.

"Why'n't you go ahead?"

Penrod, after waiting in keen suspense, turned
to behold his friend standing with his right arm
above his head, his left hand over his left ear, and
both eyes closed.

"I can't pull the trigger," said Sam indistinctly,
his face convulsed as in sympathy with the great

muscular efforts of other parts of his body. "She won't pull!"

"She won't?" Penrod remarked with scorn. "I'll bet *I* could pull her."

Sam promptly opened his eyes and handed the weapon to Penrod.

"All right," he said, with surprising and unusual mildness. "You try her, then."

Inwardly discomfited to a disagreeable extent, Penrod attempted to talk his own misgivings out of countenance.

"Poor 'ittle baby!" he said, swinging the pistol at his side with a fair pretense of careless ease. "Ain't even strong enough to pull a trigger! Poor 'ittle baby! Well, if you can't even do that much, you better watch me while *I*——"

"Well," said Sam reasonably, "why don't you go on and do it then?"

"Well, I *am* goin' to, ain't I?"

"Well, then, why don't you?"

"Oh, I'll do it fast enough to suit *you*, I guess," Penrod retorted, swinging the big revolver up a little higher than his shoulder and pointing it in the direction of the double doors, which opened upon the alley. "You better run, Sam," he jeered.

"'I can't pull the trigger,' said Sam indistinctly.
'She won't pull!'"

"You'll be pretty scared when I shoot her off, I guess."

"Well, why don't you *see* if I will?   I bet you're afraid yourself."

"Oh, I am, am I?" said Penrod, in a reckless voice —and his finger touched the trigger.   It seemed to him that his finger no more than touched it; perhaps he had been reassured by Sam's assertion that the trigger was difficult.   His intentions must remain in doubt, and probably Penrod himself was not certain of them; but one thing comes to the surface as entirely definite—that trigger was not so hard to pull as Sam said it was.

Bang! Wh-a-a-ack   A shattering report split the air of the stable, and there was an orifice of re-markable diameter in the alley door.   With these phenomena, three yells, expressing excitement of different kinds, were almost simultaneous—two from within the stable and the third from a point in the alley about eleven inches lower than the orifice just constructed in the planking of the door.   This third point, roughly speaking, was the open mouth of a gayly dressed young coloured man whose attention, as he strolled, had been thus violently distracted from some mental computations he was making in numbers, including, particularly, those symbols of ecstasy or woe, as the case might be, seven and eleven. His eye at once perceived the orifice on a line enervatingly little above the top of his head; and, although he had not supposed himself so well known in this neighbourhood, he was aware that he did, here and there, possess acquaintances of whom some such uncomplimentary action might be expected as natural and characteristic. His immediate procedure was to prostrate himself flat upon the ground, against the stable doors.

In so doing, his shoulders came brusquely in contact with one of them, which happened to be unfastened, and it swung open, revealing to his gaze two stark-white white boys, one of them holding an enormous pistol and both staring at him in stupor of ultimate horror. For, to the glassy eyes of Penrod and Sam, the stratagem of the young coloured man, thus dropping to earth, disclosed, with awful certainty, a slaughtered body.

This dreadful thing raised itself upon its elbows and looked at them, and there followed a motionless moment—a tableau of brief duration, for both boys turned and would have fled, shrieking, but the body spoke:

"'At's a nice business!" it said reproachfully. "Nice business! Tryin' blow a man's head off!"

Penrod was unable to speak, but Sam managed to summon the tremulous semblance of a voice.

"Where—where did it hit you?" he gasped.

"Nemmine anything 'bout where it *hit* me," the young coloured man returned, dusting his breast and knees as he rose. "I want to know what kine o' white boys you think you is—man can't walk 'long street 'thout you blowin' his head off!" He entered the stable and, with an indignation surely justified, took the pistol from the limp, cold hand of Penrod. "Whose gun you playin' with? Where you git 'at gun?"

"It's ours," quavered Sam. "It belongs to us."

"Then you' pa ought to be 'rested," said the young coloured man. "Lettin' boys p ay with gun!" He examined the revolver with an interest in which there began to appear symptoms of a pleasurable appreciation. "My goo'ness! Gun like 'iss blow a team o' steers thew a brick house! *Look* at 'at gun!" With his right hand he twirled it in a manner most dexterous and surprising; then suddenly he became severe. "You white boy, listen me!" he said. "Ef I went an did what I *ought* to did, I'd march straight

out 'iss stable, git a policeman, an' tell him 'rest you
an' take you off to jail. 'At's what you need—
blowin' man's head off! Listen me: I'm goin' take
'iss gun an' th'ow her away where you can't do no
mo' harm with her. I'm goin' take her way off_in
the woods an' th'ow her away where can't nobody
fine her an' go blowin' man's head off with her.
'At's what I'm goin' do!" And placing the revolver
inside his coat as inconspicuously as possible, he
proceeded to the open door and into the alley, where
he turned for a final word. "I let you off 'iss one
time," he said, "but listen me—you listen, white boy:
you bet' not tell you' pa. *I* ain' goin' tell him, an'
you ain' goin' tell him. He want know where gun
gone, you tell him you los' her."

He disappeared rapidly.

Sam Williams, swallowing continuously, presently
walked to the alley door, and remarked in a weak
voice, "I'm sick at my stummick." He paused,
then added more decidedly: "I'm goin' home. I
guess I've stood about enough around here for one
day!" And bestowing a last glance upon his friend,
who was now sitting dumbly upon the floor in the
exact spot where he had stood to fire the dreadful
shot, Sam moved slowly away.

The early shades of autumn evening were falling when Penrod emerged from the stable; and a better light might have disclosed to a shrewd eye some indications that here was a boy who had been extremely, if temporarily, ill. He went to the cistern, and, after a cautious glance round the reassuring horizon, lifted the iron cover. Then he took from the inner pocket of his jacket an object which he dropped listlessly into the water: it was a bit of wood, whittled to the likeness of a pistol. And though his lips moved not, nor any sound issued from his vocal organs, yet were words formed. They were so deep in the person of Penrod they came almost from the slowly convalescing profundities of his stomach. These words concerned firearms, and they were:

"Wish I'd never seen one! Never want to see one again!"

Of course Penrod had no way of knowing that, as regards bingism in general, several of the most distinguished old gentlemen in Europe were at that very moment in exactly the same state of mind.

CHAPTER V

THE IN-OR-IN

GEORGIE BASSETT was a boy set apart. Not only that; Georgie knew that he was a boy set apart. He would think about it for ten or twenty minutes at a time, and he could not look at himself in a mirror and remain wholly without emotion. What that emotion was, he would have been unable to put into words, but it helped him to understand that there was a certain noble something about him which other boys did not possess.

Georgie's mother had been the first to discover that Georgie was a boy set apart. In fact, Georgie did not know it until one day, when he happened to overhear his mother telling two of his aunts about it. True, he had always understood that he was the best boy in town and he intended to be a minister when he grew up, but he had never before comprehended the full extent of his sanctity, and, from that fraught moment onward, he had an almost theatrical sense of his set-apartness.

Penrod Schofield and Sam Williams and the other
boys of the neighbourhood all were conscious that
there was something different and spiritual about
Georgie, and, though this consciousness of theirs
may have been a little obscure, it was none the less
actual. That is to say, they knew that Georgie
Bassett was a boy set apart, but they did not know
that they knew it. Georgie's air and manner at
all times demonstrated to them that the thing was
so, and, moreover, their mothers absorbed appreciation of Georgie's wonderfulness from the very
fount of it, for Mrs. Bassett's conversation was of
little else. Thus, the radiance of his character became the topic of envious parental comment during
moments of strained patience in many homes, so
that altogether the most remarkable fact to be
stated of Georgie Bassett is that he escaped the consequences as long as he did.

Strange as it may seem, no actual violence was
done him except upon the incidental occasion of a
tar-fight, into which he was drawn by an obvious
eccentricity on the part of destiny. Naturally, he
was not popular with his comrades; in all games he
was pushed aside, and disregarded, being invariably
the tail-ender in every pastime in which leaders

"chose sides"; his counsels were slighted as worse than weightless, and all his opinions instantly hooted. Still, ·considering the circumstances fairly and thoughtfully, it is difficult to deny that his boy companions showed creditable moderation in their treatment of him. That is, they were moderate up to a certain date, and even then they did not directly attack him—there was nothing cold-blooded about it at all. The thing was forced upon them, and, though they all felt pleased and uplifted—while it was happening—they did not understand precisely why. Nothing could more clearly prove their innocence of heart than this very ignorance, and yet none of the grown people who later felt themselves concerned in the matter was able to look at it in that light. Now, here was a characteristic working of those reactions which produce what is sometimes called "the injustice of life," because the grown people were responsible for the whole affair and were really the guilty parties. It was from grown people that Georgie Bassett learned that he was a boy set apart, and the effect upon him was what alienated his friends. Then these alienated friends were brought (by odious comparisons on the part of grown people) to a condition of mind wherein they suffered dumb annoyance, like a low fever, whenever they heard Georgie's name mentioned, while association with his actual person became every day more and more irritating. And yet, having laid this fuse and having kept it constantly glowing, the grown people expected nothing to happen to Georgie.

The catastrophe befell as a consequence of Sam Williams deciding to have a shack in his backyard. Sam had somehow obtained a vasty piano-box and a quantity of lumber, and, summoning Penrod Schofield and the coloured brethren, Herman and Verman, he expounded to them his building-plans and offered them shares and benefits in the institution he purposed to found. Acceptance was enthusiastic; straightway the assembly became a union of carpenters all of one mind, and ten days saw the shack not completed but comprehensible. Anybody could tell, by that time, that it was intended for a shack.

There was a door on leather hinges; it drooped, perhaps, but it was a door. There was a window— not a glass one, but, at least, it could be "looked out of," as Sam said. There was a chimney made of stovepipe, though that was merely decorative, because the cooking was done out of doors in an underground "furnace" which the boys excavated. There were pictures pasted on the interior walls, and, hanging from a nail, there was a crayon portrait of Sam's grandfather, which he had brought down from the attic quietly, though, as he said, it "wasn't any use on earth up there." There were two lame chairs from Penrod's attic, and along one wall ran a low and feeble structure intended to serve as a bench or divan. This would come in handy, Sam said, if any of the party "had to lay down or anything," and at a pinch (such as a meeting of the association) it would serve to seat all the members in a row.

For, coincidentally with the development of the shack, the builders became something more than partners. Later, no one could remember who first suggested the founding of a secret order, or society, as a measure of exclusiveness and to keep the shack sacred to members only, but it was an idea that presently began to be more absorbing and satisfactory than even the shack itself. The outward manifestations of it might have been observed in the increased solemnity and preoccupation of the Caucasian members and in a few ceremonial observances exposed to the public eye. As an instance of these latter, Mrs. Williams, happening to glance from a rearward window, about four o'clock one afternoon, found her attention arrested by what seemed to be a flag-raising before the door of the shack. Sam and Herman and Verman stood in attitudes of rigid attention, shoulder to shoulder, while Penrod Schofield, facing them, was apparently delivering some sort of exhortation which he read from a scribbled sheet of foolscap. Concluding this, he lifted from the ground a long and somewhat warped clothes-prop, from one end of which hung a whitish flag, or pennon, bearing an inscription. Sam and Herman and Verman lifted their right hands, while Penrod placed the other end of the clothes-prop in a hole in the ground, with the pennon fluttering high above the shack. He then raised his own right hand, and the four boys repeated something in concert. It was inaudible to Mrs. Williams, but she was able to make out the inscription upon the pennon. It consisted of the peculiar phrase, "In-Or-In," done in black paint upon a muslin ground, and consequently seeming to be in need of a blotter.

It recurred to her mind, later that evening, when she happened to find herself alone with Sam in the library, and, in merest idle curiosity, she asked:

"Sam, what does 'In-Or-In' mean?"

Sam, bending over an arithmetic, uncreased his brow till it became of a blank and marble smoothness.

"Ma'am?"

"What are those words on your flag?"

Sam gave her a long, cold, mystic look, rose to his feet, and left the room with emphasis and dignity. For a moment she was puzzled. But Sam's older brother was this year completing his education at a university, and Mrs. Williams was not altogether ignorant of the obligations of secrecy imposed upon some brotherhoods; so she was able to comprehend Sam's silent withdrawal, and, instead of summoning him back for further questions, she waited until he was out of hearing and then began to laugh.

Sam's action was in obedience to one of the rules adopted, at his own suggestion, as a law of the order. Penrod advocated it warmly. From Margaret he had heard accounts of her friends in college and thus had learned much that ought to be done. On the other hand, Herman subscribed to it with reluctance, expressing a decided opinion that if he and Verman were questioned upon the matter at home and adopted the line of conduct required by the new rule, it

would be well for them to depart not only from the
room in which the questioning took place but from the
house, and hurriedly at that.   "An' *stay* away!" he
concluded.

Verman, being tongue-tied—not without advantage in this case, and surely an ideal qualification for
membership—was not so apprehensive.   He voted
with Sam and Penrod, carrying the day.

New rules were adopted at every meeting (though
it cannot be said that all of them were practicable)
for, in addition to the information possessed by
Sam and Penrod, Herman and Verman had many
ideas of their own, founded upon remarks overheard
at home.   Both their parents belonged to secret
orders, their father to the Innapenent 'Nevolent
Lodge (so stated by Herman) and their mother to
the Order of White Doves.

From these and other sources, Penrod found no
difficulty in compiling material for what came to
be known as the "rixual"; and it was the rixual he
was reading to the members when Mrs. Williams
happened to observe the ceremonial raising of the
emblem of the order.

The rixual contained the oath, a key to the secret
language, or code (devised by Penrod for use in

uncertain emergencies), and passwords for admission to the shack, also instructions for recognizing a brother member in the dark, and a rather alarming sketch of the things to be done during the initiation of a candidate.

This last was employed for the benefit of Master Roderick Magsworth Bitts, Junior, on the Saturday following the flag-raising. He presented himself in Sam's yard, not for initiation, indeed—having no previous knowledge of the Society of the In-Or-In— but for general purposes of sport and pastime. At first sight of the shack he expressed anticipations of pleasure, adding some suggestions for improving the architectural effect. Being prevented, however, from entering, and even from standing in the vicinity of the sacred building, he plaintively demanded an explanation; whereupon he was commanded to withdraw to the front yard for a time, and the members held meeting in the shack. Roddy was elected, and consented to undergo the initiation.

He was not the only new member that day. A short time after Roddy had been taken into the shack for the reading of the rixual and other ceremonies, little Maurice Levy entered the Williams' gate and strolled round to the backyard, looking for

Sam. He was surprised and delighted to behold the promising shack, and, like Roddy, entertained fair hopes for the future.

The door of the shack was closed; a board covered the window, but a murmur of voices came from within. Maurice stole close and listened. Through a crack he could see the flicker of a candle-flame, and he heard the voice of Penrod Schofield:

"Roddy Bitts, do you solemnly swear?"

"Well, all right," said the voice of Roddy, somewhat breathless.

"How many fingers you see before your eyes?"

"Can't see any," Roddy returned. "How could I, with this thing over my eyes, and laying down on my stummick, anyway?"

"Then the time has come," Penrod announced in solemn tones. "The time has come."

Whack!

Evidently a broad and flat implement was thereupon applied to Roddy.

"*Ow !*" complained the candidate.

"No noise!" said Penrod sternly, and added: "Roddy Bitts must now say the oath. Say exackly what I say, Roddy, and if you don't—well, you better, because you'll see! Now, say 'I solemnly swear——'"

"I solemnly swear——" said Roddy.

"To keep the secrets——"

"To keep the secrets——" Roddy repeated.

"To keep the secrets in infadelaty and violate and sanctuary."

"What?" Roddy naturally inquired.

Whack!

"*Ow!*" cried Roddy. "That's no fair!"

"You got to say just what *I* say," Penrod was heard informing him. "That's the rixual, and anyway, even if you do get it right, Verman's got to hit you every now and then, because that's part of the rixual, too. Now go on and say it. 'I solemnly swear to keep the secrets in infadelaty and violate and sanctuary.'"

"I solemnly swear——" Roddy began.

But Maurice Levy was tired of being no party to such fascinating proceedings, and he began to hammer upon the door.

"Sam! Sam Williams!" he shouted. "Lemme in there! I know lots about 'nishiatin'. Lemme in!"

The door was flung open, revealing Roddy Bitts, blindfolded and bound, lying face down upon the floor of the shack; but Maurice had only a fugitive glimpse of this pathetic figure before he, too, was recumbent. Four boys flung themselves indignantly upon him and bore him to earth.

"Hi!" he squealed. "What you doin'? Haven't you got any *sense ?*"

And, from within the shack, Roddy added his own protest.

"Let me up, can't you?" he cried. "I got to see what's goin' on out there, haven't I? I guess I'm not goin' to lay here all *day !* What you think I'm made of?"

"You hush up!" Penrod commanded. "This is a nice biznuss!" he continued, deeply aggrieved. "What kind of a 'nishiation do you expect this is, anyhow?"

"Well, here's Maurice Levy gone and seen part of the secrets," said Sam, in a voice of equal plaintiveness. "Yes; and I bet he was listenin' out here, too!"

"Lemme up!" begged Maurice, half stifled. "I didn't do any harm to your old secrets, did I? Anyways, I just as soon be 'nishiated myself. I ain't afraid. So if you 'nishiate me, what difference will it make if I did hear a little?"

Struck with this idea, which seemed reasonable,

Penrod obtained silence from every one except Roddy, and it was decided to allow Maurice to rise and retire to the front yard. The brother members then withdrew within the shack, elected Maurice to the fellowship, and completed the initiation of Mr. Bitts. After that, Maurice was summoned and underwent the ordeal with fortitude, though the newest brother—still tingling with his own experiences—helped to make certain parts of the rixual unprecedentedly severe.

Once endowed with full membership, Maurice and Roddy accepted the obligations and privileges of the order with enthusiasm. Both interested themselves immediately in improvements for the shack, and made excursions to their homes to obtain materials. Roddy returned with a pair of lensless mother-of-pearl opera-glasses, a contribution which led to the creation of a new office, called the "warner." It was his duty to climb upon the back fence once every fifteen minutes and search the horizon for intruders or "anybody that hasn't got any biznuss around here." This post proved so popular, at first, that it was found necessary to provide for rotation in office, and to shorten the interval from fifteen minutes to an indefinite but much briefer period, determined principally by argument between the incumbent and his successor.

And Maurice Levy contributed a device so pleasant, and so necessary to the prevention of interruption during meetings, that Penrod and Sam wondered why they had not thought of it themselves long before. It consisted of about twenty-five feet of garden hose in fair condition. One end of it was introduced into the shack through a knothole, and the other was secured by wire round the faucet of hydrant in the stable. Thus, if members of the order were assailed by thirst during an important session, or in the course of an initiation, it would not be necessary for them all to leave the shack. One could go, instead, and when he had turned on the water at the hydrant, the members in the shack could drink without leaving their places. It was discovered, also, that the section of hose could be used as a speaking-tube; and though it did prove necessary to explain by shouting outside the tube what one had said into it, still there was a general feeling that it provided another means of secrecy and an additional safeguard against intrusion. It is true that during the half-hour immediately following the installation of this convenience, there

was a little violence among the brothers concerning
a question of policy. Sam, Roddy, and Verman—
Verman especially—wished to use the tube "to talk
through," and Maurice, Penrod, and Herman wished
to use it "to drink through." As a consequence of the
success of the latter party, the shack became too damp
for habitation until another day, and several members,
as they went home at dusk, might easily have been
mistaken for survivors of some marine catastrophe.

Still, not every shack is equipped with running
water, and exuberance befitted the occasion. Everybody agreed that the afternoon had been one of
the most successful and important in many weeks.
The Order of the In-Or-In was doing splendidly;
and yet every brother felt, in his heart, that there
was one thing that could spoil it. Against that
fatality, all were united to protect themselves, the
shack, the rixual, the opera-glasses, and the water-
and-speaking tube. Sam spoke not only for himself but for the entire order when he declared, in
speeding the last parting guest:

"Well, we got to stick to one thing or we might as
well quit! *Georgie Bassett* better not come pokin'
around!"

"No, *sir!*" said Penrod,

CHAPTER VI

GEORGIE BECOMES A MEMBER

BUT Georgie did. It is difficult to imagine how cause and effect could be more closely and patiently related. Inevitably, Georgie did come poking around. How was he to refrain when daily, up and down the neighbourhood, the brothers strutted with mystic and important airs, when they whispered together and uttered words of strange import in his presence? Thus did they defeat their own object. They desired to keep Georgie at a distance, yet they could not refrain from posing before him. They wished to impress upon him the fact that he was an outsider, and they but succeeded in rousing his desire to be an insider, a desire which soon became a determination. For few were the days until he not only knew of the shack but had actually paid it a visit. That was upon a morning when the other boys were in school, Georgie having found himself indisposed until about ten o'clock, when he was able to take nourishment

and subsequently to interest himself in this rather
private errand. He climbed the Williams' alley
fence, and having made a modest investigation of
the exterior of the shack, which was padlocked, retired without having disturbed anything except his
own peace of mind. His curiosity, merely piqued
before, now became ravenous and painful. It was
not allayed by the mystic manners of the members
or by the unnecessary emphasis they laid upon their
coldness toward himself; and when a committee
informed him darkly that there were "secret orders"
to prevent his coming within "a hundred and six-
teen feet"—such was Penrod's arbitrary language
—of the Williams' yard, "in any direction," Georgie
could bear it no longer, but entered his own house,
and, in burning words, laid the case before a woman
higher up. Here the responsibility for things is
directly traceable to grown people. Within that
hour, Mrs. Bassett sat in Mrs. Williams' library
to address her hostess upon the subject of Georgie's
grievance.

"Of course, it isn't Sam's fault," she said, concluding her interpretation of the affair. "Georgie likes
Sam, and didn't blame him at all. No; we both
felt that Sam would always be a polite, nice boy—

Georgie used those very words—but Penrod seems to have a *very* bad influence.   Georgie felt that Sam would *want* him to come and play in the shack if Penrod didn't make Sam do everything *he* wants. What hurt Georgie most is that it's *Sam's* shack, and he felt for another boy to come and tell him that he mustn't even go *near* it—well, of course, it was very trying.   And he's very much hurt with little Maurice Levy, too.   He said that he was sure that even Penrod would be glad to have him for a member of their little club if it weren't for Maurice —and I think he spoke of Roddy Bitts, too."

The fact that the two remaining members were coloured was omitted from this discourse—which leads to the deduction that Georgie had not mentioned it.

"Georgie said all the other boys liked him very much," Mrs. Bassett continued, "and that he felt it his duty to join the club, because most of them were so anxious to have him, and he is sure he would have a good influence over them.   He really did speak of it in quite a touching way, Mrs. Williams. Of course, we mothers mustn't brag of our sons too much, but Georgie *really* isn't like other boys.   He is so sensitive, you can't think how this little affair has hurt him, and I felt that it might even make him ill. You see, I *had* to respect his reason for wanting to join the club. And if I *am* his mother" —she gave a deprecating little laugh—"I must say that it seems noble to want to join not really for his own sake but for the good that he felt his influence would have over the other boys. Don't you think so, Mrs. Williams?"

Mrs. Williams said that she did, indeed. And the result of this interview was another, which took place between Sam and his father that evening, for Mrs. Williams, after talking to Sam herself, felt that the matter needed a man to deal with it. The man did it man-fashion.

"You either invite Georgie Bassett to play in the shack all he wants to," said the man, "or the shack comes down."

"But——"

"Take your choice. I'm not going to have neighbourhood quarrels over such——"

"But, papa——"

"That's enough! You said yourself you haven't anything against Georgie."

"I said——"

"You said you didn't like him, but you couldn't

tell why. You couldn't state a single instance of
bad behaviour against him. You couldn't mention
anything he ever did which wasn't what a gentleman
should have done. It's no use, I tell you. Either
you invite Georgie to play in the shack as much as
he likes next Saturday, or the shack comes down."

"But, *papa*——"

"I'm not going to talk any more about it. If you
want the shack pulled down and hauled away, you
and your friends continue to tantalize this inoffensive
little boy the way you have been. If you want to
keep it, be polite and invite him in."

"But——"

"That's *ALL*, I said!"

Sam was crushed.

Next day he communicated the bitter substance
of the edict to the other members, and gloom became
unanimous. So serious an aspect did the affair
present that it was felt necessary to call a special
meeting of the order after school. The entire membership was in attendance; the door was closed, the
window covered with a board, and the candle lighted.
Then all of the brothers—except one—began to
express their sorrowful apprehensions. The whole
thing was spoiled, they agreed, if Georgie Bassett

had to be taken in. On the other hand, if they didn't take him in, "there wouldn't be anything left." The one brother who failed to express any opinion was little Verman. He was otherwise occupied.

Verman had been the official paddler during the initiations of Roddy Bitts and Maurice Levy; his work had been conscientious, and it seemed to be taken by consent that he was to continue in office. An old shingle from the woodshed roof had been used for the exercise of his function in the cases of Roddy and Maurice, but this afternoon he had brought with him a new one, which he had picked up somewhere. It was broader and thicker than the old one, and, during the melancholy prophecies of his fellows, he whittled the lesser end of it to the likeness of a handle. Thus engaged, he bore no appearance of despondency; on the contrary, his eyes, shining brightly in the candlelight, indicated that eager thoughts possessed him, while from time to time the sound of a chuckle issued from his simple African throat. Gradually the other brothers began to notice his preoccupation, and one by one they fell silent, regarding him thoughtfully. Slowly the darkness of their countenances lifted a little; something happier and brighter began to glimmer from each boyish face. All eyes remained fascinated upon Verman.

"Well, anyway," said Penrod, in a tone that was almost cheerful, "this is only Tuesday. We got pretty near all week to fix up the 'nishiation for Saturday."

And Saturday brought sunshine to make the occasion more tolerable for both the candidate and the society. Mrs. Williams, going to the window to watch Sam, when he left the house after lunch, marked with pleasure that his look and manner were sprightly as he skipped down the walk to the front gate. There he paused and yodelled for a time. An answering yodel came presently; Penrod Schofield appeared, and by his side walked Georgie Bassett. Georgie was always neat, but Mrs. Williams noticed that he exhibited unusual gloss and polish to-day. As for his expression, it was a shade too complacent under the circumstances, though, for that matter, perfect tact avoids an air of triumph under any circumstances. Mrs. Williams was pleased to observe that Sam and Penrod betrayed no resentment whatever; they seemed to have accepted defeat in a good spirit and to be inclined to make the best of

Georgie. Indeed, they appeared to be genuinely excited about him—it was evident that their cordiality was eager and wholehearted.

· The three boys conferred for a few moments; then Sam disappeared round the house and returned, waving his hand and nodding. Upon that, Penrod took Georgie's left arm, Sam took his right, and the three marched off to the backyard in a companionable way which made Mrs. Williams feel that it had been an excellent thing to interfere a little in Georgie's interest.

Experiencing the benevolent warmth that comes of assisting in a good action, she ascended to an apartment upstairs, and, for a couple of hours, employed herself with needle and thread in sartorial repairs on behalf of her husband and Sam. Then she was interrupted by the advent of a coloured serving-maid.

"Miz Williams, I reckon the house goin' fall down!" said this pessimist, arriving out of breath. "That s'iety o' Mist' Sam's suttenly tryin' to pull the roof down on ow haids!"

"The roof?" Mrs. Williams inquired mildly. "They aren't in the attic, are they?"

"No'm; they in the celluh, but they *reachin'* fer

the roof! I nev' did hear no sech a rumpus an' squawkin' an' squawlin' an' fallin' an' whoopin' an' whackin' an' bangin'! They troop down by the outside celluh do', n'en—bang!—they bus' loose, an' been goin' on ev' since, wuss'n Bedlun! Ef they anything down celluh ain' broke by this time, it cain' be only jes' the foundashum, an' I bet *that* ain't goin' stan' much longer! I'd gone down an' stop 'em, but I'm 'fraid to. Hones', Miz Williams, I'm 'fraid o' my life go down there, all that Bedlun goin' on. I thought I come see what you say."

Mrs. Williams laughed.

"We'll have to stand a little noise in the house sometimes, Fanny, when there are boys. They're just playing, and a lot of noise is usually a pretty safe sign."

"Yes'm," said Fanny. "It's yo' house, Miz Williams, not mine. You want 'em tear it down, I'm willin'."

She departed, and Mrs. Williams continued to sew. The days were growing short, and at five o'clock she was obliged to put the work aside, as her eyes did not permit her to continue it by artificial light. Descending to the lower floor, she found the house silent, and when she opened the front door

to see if the evening paper had come, she beheld
Sam, Penrod, and Maurice Levy standing near the
gate engaged in quiet conversation. Penrod and
Maurice departed while she was looking for the
paper, and Sam came thoughtfully up the walk.

"Well, Sam," she said, "it wasn't such a bad thing,
after all, to show a little politeness to Georgie
Bassett, was it?"

Sam gave her a non-committal look—expression
of every kind had been wiped from his countenance.
He presented a blank surface.

"No'm," he said meekly.

"Everything was just a little pleasanter because
you'd been friendly, wasn't it?"

"Yes'm."

"Has Georgie gone home?"

"Yes'm."

"I hear you made enough noise in the cellar——
Did Georgie have a good time?"

"Ma'am?"

"Did Georgie Bassett have a good time?"

"Well"—Sam now had the air of a person trying
to remember details with absolute accuracy—"well,
he didn't say he did, and he didn't say he didn't."

"Didn't he thank the boys?"

"No'm."

"Didn't he even thank you?"

"No'm."

"Why, that's queer," she said. "He's always so polite. He *seemed* to be having a good time, didn't he, Sam?"

"Ma'am?"

"Didn't Georgie seem to be enjoying himself?"

This question, apparently so simple, was not answered with promptness. Sam looked at his mother in a puzzled way, and then he found it necessary to rub each of his shins in turn with the palm of his right hand.

"I stumbled," he said apologetically. "I stumbled on the cellar steps."

"Did you hurt yourself?" she asked quickly.

"No'm; but I guess maybe I better rub some arnica——"

"I'll get it," she said. "Come up to your father's bathroom, Sam. Does it hurt much?"

"No'm," he answered truthfully, "it hardly hurts at all."

And having followed her to the bathroom, he insisted, with unusual gentleness, that he be left to apply the arnica to the alleged injuries himself.

He was so persuasive that she yielded, and descended
to the library, where she found her husband once
more at home after his day's work.

"Well?" he said. "Did Georgie show up, and
were they decent to him?"

"Oh, yes; it's all right. Sam and Penrod were
good as gold. I saw them being actually cordial
to him."

"That's well," said Mr. Williams, settling into a
chair with his paper. "I was a little apprehensive,
but I suppose I was mistaken. I walked home, and
just now, as I passed Mrs. Bassett's, I saw Doctor
Venny's car in front, and that barber from the
corner shop on Second Street was going in the door.
I couldn't think what a widow would need a barber
and a doctor for—especially at the same time. I
couldn't think what Georgie'd need such a combi-
nation for either, and then I got afraid that maybe——"

Mrs. Williams laughed. "Oh, no; it hasn't anything to do with his having been over here. I'm sure
they were very nice to him."

"Well, I'm glad of that."

"Yes, indeed——" Mrs. Williams began, when
Fanny appeared, summoning her to the telephone.

It is pathetically true that Mrs. Williams went to

the telephone humming a little song. She was detained at the instrument not more than five minutes; then she made a plunging return into the library, a blanched and stricken woman. She made strange, sinister gestures at her husband.

He sprang up, miserably prophetic.

"Mrs. Bassett?"

"Go to the telephone," Mrs. Williams said hoarsely, "She wants to talk to you, too. She *can't* talk much—she's hysterical. She says they lured Georgie into the cellar and had him beaten by negroes! That's not all——"

Oh my!

Mr. Williams was already on his way.

"You find Sam!" he commanded, over his shoulder.

Mrs. Williams stepped into the front hall.

"Sam!" she called, addressing the upper reaches of the stairway. "Sam!"

Not even echo answered.

"*Sam!*"

A faint clearing of somebody's throat was heard behind her, a sound so modest and unobtrusive it was no more than just audible, and, turning, the mother beheld her son sitting upon the floor in the shadow of the stairs and gazing meditatively at

the hatrack. His manner indicated that he wished
to produce the impression that he had been sitting
there, in this somewhat unusual place and occupation, for a considerable time, but without over-
hearing anything that went on in the library - so
close by.

"Sam," she cried, "what have you *done* ?"

"Well—I guess my legs are all right," he said
gently. "I got the arnica on, so probably they
won't hurt any m——"

"Stand up!" she said.

"Ma'am?"

"March into the library!"

Sam marched—slow-time. In fact, no funeral
march has been composed in a time so slow as to
suit this march of Sam's. One might have suspected
that he was in a state of apprehension.

Mr. Williams entered at one door as his son
crossed the threshold of the other, and this encounter
was a piteous sight. After one glance at his father's
face, Sam turned desperately, as if to flee outright.
But Mrs. Williams stood in the doorway behind him.

"You come here!" And the father's voice was as
terrible as his face. "*What did you do to Georgie
Bassett ?*"

"Nothin'," Sam gulped; "nothin' at all."

"What!"

"We just—we just 'nishiated him."

Mr. Williams turned abruptly, walked to the fireplace, and there turned again, facing the wretched Sam.

"That's all you did?"

"Yes, sir."

"Georgie Bassett's mother has just told me over the telephone," said Mr. Williams deliberately, "that you and Penrod Schofield and Roderick Bitts and Maurice Levy *lured Georgie into the cellar and had him beaten by negroes !*"

At this, Sam was able to hold up his head a little and to summon a rather feeble indignation.

"It ain't so," he declared. "We didn't any such thing lower him into the cellar. We weren't goin' *near* the cellar with him. We never *thought* of goin' down cellar. He went down there himself, first."

"So! I suppose he was running away from you, poor thing! Trying to escape from you, wasn't he?"

"He wasn't," said Sam doggedly. "We weren't chasin' him—or anything at all."

"Then why did he go in the cellar?"

"Well, he didn't exactly *go* in the cellar," said Sam reluctantly.

"Well, how did he *get* in the cellar, then?"

"He—he fell in," said Sam.

"*How* did he fall in?"

"Well, the door was open, and—well, he kept walkin' around there, and we hollered at him to keep away, but just then he kind of—well, the first *I* noticed was I couldn't *see* him, and so we went and looked down the steps, and he was sitting down there on the bottom step and kind of shouting, and——"

"See here!" Mr. Williams interrupted. "You're going to make a clean breast of this whole affair and take the consequences. You're going to tell it and tell it *all*. Do you understand that?"

"Yes, sir."

"Then you tell me how Georgie Bassett fell down the cellar steps—and tell me quick!"

"He—he was blindfolded."

"Aha! *Now* we're getting at it. You begin at the beginning and tell me just what you did to him from the time he got here. Understand?"

"Yes, sir."

"Go on, then!"

"Well, I'm goin' to," Sam protested. "We never hurt him at all. He wasn't even hurt when he fell down cellar. There's a lot of mud down there, because the cellar door leaks, and——"

"Sam!" Mr. Williams's tone was deadly. "Did you hear me tell you to begin at the beginning?"

Sam made a great effort and was able to obey.

"Well, we had everything ready for the 'nishiation before lunch," he said. "We wanted it all to be nice, because you said we had to have him, papa, and after lunch Penrod went to guard him— that's a new part in the rixual—and he brought him over, and we took him out to the shack and blindfolded him, and—well, he got kind of mad because we wanted him to lay down on his stummick and be tied up, and he said he wouldn't, because the floor was a little bit wet in there and he could feel it sort of squashy under his shoes, and he said his mother didn't want him ever to get dirty and he just wouldn't do it; and we all kept telling him he had to, or else how could there be any 'nishiation; and he kept gettin' madder and said he wanted to have the 'nishiation outdoors where it wasn't wet and he wasn't goin' to lay down on his stummick, anyway." Sam paused for wind, then got under way again:

"Well, some of the boys were tryin' to get him to
lay down on his stummick, and he kind of fell up
against the door and it came open and he ran out
in the yard. He was tryin' to get the blindfold off
his eyes, but he couldn't, because it was a towel-in
a pretty hard knot; and he went tearin' all around
the backyard, and we didn't chase him, or anything.
All we did was just watch him—and that's when he
fell in the cellar. Well, it didn't hurt him any. It
didn't hurt him at all, but he was muddier than
what he would of been if he'd just had sense enough
to lay down in the shack. Well, so we thought,
long as he was down in the cellar anyway, we might
as well have the rest of the 'nishiation down there.
So we brought the things down and—and 'nishiated
him—and that's all. That's every bit we did to
him."

"Yes," said Mr. Williams sardonically; "I see.
What were the details of the initiation?"

"Sir?"

"I want to know what else you did to him? What
was the initiation?"

"It's—it's secret," Sam murmured piteously.

"Not any longer, I assure you! The society is a
thing of the past and you'll find your friend Pen-

rod's parents agree with me in that. Mrs. Bassett
had already telephoned them when she called us
up. You go on with your story!"

Sam sighed deeply, and yet it may have been a
consolation to know that his present misery was
not altogether without its counterpart. Through
the falling dusk his spirit may have crossed the
intervening distance to catch a glimpse of his friend
suffering simultaneously and standing within the
same peril. And if Sam's spirit did thus behold
Penrod in jeopardy, it was a true vision.

"Go on!" said Mr. Williams.

"Well, there wasn't any fire in the furnace because it's too warm yet, and we weren't goin' to do
anything'd *hurt* him, so we put him in there——"

"In the *furnace* ?"

"It was cold," protested Sam. "There hadn't
been any fire there since last spring. Course we
told him there was fire in it. We *had* to do that,"
he continued earnestly, "because that was part of
the 'nishiation. We only kept him in it a little
while and kind of hammered on the outside a little,
and then we took him out and got him to lay down
on his stummick, because he was all muddy anyway,
where he fell down the cellar; and how could it

matter to anybody that had any sense at all? Well, then we had the rixual, and—and—why, the teeny little paddlin' he got wouldn't hurt a flea! It was that little coloured boy lives in the alley did it—he isn't anyways near *half* Georgie's size—but Georgie got mad and said he didn't want any ole nigger to paddle him. That's what he said, and it was his own foolishness, because Verman won't let *anybody* call him 'nigger,' and if Georgie was goin' to call him that, he ought to had sense enough not to do it when he was layin' down that way and Verman all ready to be the paddler. And he needn't of been so mad at the rest of us, either, because it took us about twenty minutes to get the paddle away from Verman after that, and we had to lock Verman up in the laundry-room and not let him out till it was all over. Well, and then things were kind of spoiled, anyway; so we didn't do but just a little more—and that's all."

"Go on! What was the 'just a little more?'"

"Well—we got him to swaller a little teeny bit of asafidity that Penrod used to have to wear in a bag around his neck. It wasn't enough to even make a person sneeze—it wasn't much more'n a half a spoonful—it wasn't hardly a *quarter* of a spoonf——"

"'Well, then we had, rixual, and—and—why, the teeny little paddlin'
he got wouldn't hurt a flea!'"

"Ha!" said Mr. Williams. "That accounts for the doctor. What else?"

"Well—we—we had some paint left over from our flag, and we put just a little teeny bit of it on his hair and——"

"Ha!" said Mr. Williams. "That accounts for the barber. What else?"

"That's all," said Sam, swallowing. "Then he got mad and went home."

Mr. Williams walked to the door, and sternly motioned to the culprit to precede him through it. But just before the pair passed from her sight, Mrs. Williams gave way to an uncontrollable impulse.

"Sam," she asked, "what does 'In-Or-In' stand for?"

The unfortunate boy had begun to sniffle.

"It—it means—Innapenent Order of Infadelaty," he moaned—and plodded onward to his doom.

Not his alone: at that very moment Master Roderick Magsworth Bitts, Junior, was suffering also, consequent upon telephoning on the part of Mrs. Bassett, though Roderick's punishment was administered less on the ground of Georgie's troubles and more on that of Roddy's having affiliated with an order consisting so largely of Herman and Ver-

man. As for Maurice Levy, he was no whit less unhappy. He fared as ill.

Simultaneously, two ex-members of the In-Or-In
were finding their lot fortunate. Something had
prompted them to linger in the alley in the vicinity
of the shack, and it was to this fated edifice that Mr.
Williams, with demoniac justice, brought Sam for
the deed he had in mind.

Herman and Verman listened—awe-stricken—
to what went on within the shack. Then, before
it was over, they crept away and down the alley
toward their own home. This was directly across
the alley from the Schofields' stable, and they were
horrified at the sounds which issued from the interior
of the stable store-room. It was the St. Bartholo-
mew's Eve of that neighbourhood.

"Man, man!" said Herman, shaking his head.
"Glad I ain' no white boy!"

Verman seemed gloomily to assent.

CHAPTER VII

WHITEY

PENROD and Sam made a gloomy discovery one morning in mid-October. All the week had seen amiable breezes and fair skies until Saturday, when, about breakfast-time, the dome of heaven filled solidly with gray vapour and began to drip. The boys' discovery was that there is no justice about the weather.

They sat in the carriage-house of the Schofields' empty stable; the doors upon the alley were open, and Sam and Penrod stared torpidly at the thin but implacable drizzle which was the more irritating because there was barely enough of it to interfere with a number of things they had planned to do.

"Yes; this is *nice !*" Sam said, in a tone of plaintive sarcasm. "This is a *perty* way to do!" (He was alluding to the personal spitefulness of the elements.) "I'd like to know what's the sense of it—ole sun pourin' down every day in the week when nobody needs it, then cloud up and rain all Saturday! My father said it's goin' to be a three days' rain."

"Well, nobody with any sense cares if it rains Sunday and Monday," said Penrod. "I wouldn't care if it rained every Sunday as long I lived;-but I just like to know what's the reason it had to go and rain to-day. Got all the days o' the week to choose from and goes and picks on Saturday. That's a fine biz'nuss!"

"Well, in vacation——" Sam began, but at a sound from a source invisible to him he paused. "What's that?" he said, somewhat startled.

It was a curious sound, loud and hollow and un-human, yet it seemed to be a cough. Both boys rose, and Penrod asked uneasily:

"Where'd that noise come from?"

"It's in the alley," said Sam.

Perhaps if the day had been bright, both of them would have stepped immediately to the alley doors to investigate; but their actual procedure was to move a little distance in the opposite direction. The strange cough sounded again.

"*Say !*" Penrod quavered. "What *is* that?"

Then both boys uttered smothered exclamations and jumped, for the long, gaunt head which appeared

in the doorway was entirely unexpected. It was
the cavernous and melancholy head of an incredibly
thin, old, whitish horse. This head waggled slowly
from side to side; the nostrils vibrated; the mouth
opened, and the hollow cough sounded again.

Recovering themselves, Penrod and Sam underwent the customary human reaction from alarm to
indignation.

"What you want, you ole horse, you?" Penrod
shouted. "Don't you come coughin' around *me !*"

And Sam, seizing a stick, hurled it at the intruder.

"Get out o' here!" he roared.

The aged horse nervously withdrew his head,
turned tail, and made a rickety flight up the alley,
while Sam and Penrod, perfectly obedient to inherited impulse, ran out into the drizzle and uproariously pursued. They were but automatons of
instinct, meaning no evil. Certainly they did not
know the singular and pathetic history of the old
horse who had wandered into the alley and ventured to look through the open door.

This horse, about twice the age of either Penrod
or Sam, had lived to find himself in a unique position.
He was nude, possessing neither harness nor halter;
all he had was a name, Whitey, and he would have

answered to it by a slight change of expression ·if
any one had thus properly addressed him. So for-
lorn was Whitey's case, he was actually an independent horse; he had not even an owner. For two
days and a half he had been his own master. ·_ _ _

Previous to that period he had been the property
of one Abalene Morris, a person of colour, who
would have explained himself as engaged in the
hauling business. On the contrary, the hauling
business was an insignificant side line with Mr.
Morris, for he had long ago given himself, as utterly
as fortune permitted, to that talent which, early in
youth, he had recognized as the greatest of all those
surging in his bosom. In his waking thoughts and
in his dreams, in health and in sickness, Abalene
Morris was the dashing and emotional practitioner
of an art probably more than Roman in antiquity.
Abalene was a crap-shooter. The hauling business
was a disguise.

A concentration of events had brought it about
that, at one and the same time, Abalene, after a
dazzling run of the dice, found the hauling business
an actual danger to the preservation of his liberty.
He won seventeen dollars and sixty cents, and within
the hour found himself in trouble with an officer of

the Humane Society on account of an altercation
with Whitey. Abalene had been offered four
dollars for Whitey some ten days earlier; wherefore
he at once drove to the shop of the junk-dealer who
had made the offer and announced his acquiescence
in the sacrifice.

"*No*, suh!" said the junk-dealer, with emphasis.
"I awready done got me a good mule fer my deliv'ry-
hoss, 'n'at ole Whitey hoss ain' wuff no fo' dollah
nohow! I 'uz a fool when I talk 'bout th'owin'
money roun' that a-way. *I* know what *you* up to,
Abalene. Man come by here li'l bit ago tole me all
'bout white man try to 'rest you, ovah on the
avvynoo. Yessuh; he say white man goin' to git
you yit an' th'ow you in jail 'count o' Whitey.
White man tryin' to fine out who you *is*. He say,
nemmine, he'll know Whitey ag'in, even if he don'
know you! He say he ketch you by the hoss; so
you come roun' tryin' fix me up with Whitey so
white man grab me, th'ow *me* in 'at jail. G'on
'way f'um hyuh, you Abalene! You cain' sell an'
you cain' give Whitey to no cullud man 'n 'is town.
You go an' drowned 'at ole hoss, 'cause you sutny
goin' to jail if you git ketched drivin' him."

The substance of this advice seemed good to

Abalene, especially as the seventeen dollars and sixty cents in his pocket lent sweet colours to life out of jail at this time. At dusk he led Whitey to a broad common at the edge of town, and spoke to him finally.

"G'on 'bout you biz'nis," said Abalene; "you ain' *my* hoss. Don' look roun' at me, 'cause *I* ain' got no 'quaintance wif you. I'm a man o' money, an' I got my own frien's; I'm a-lookin' fer bigger cities, hoss. You got you' biz'nis an' I got mine. Mista' Hoss, good-night!"

Whitey found a little frosted grass upon the common and remained there all night. In the morning he sought the shed where Abalene had kept him, but that was across the large and busy town, and Whitey was hopelessly lost. He had but one eye, a feeble one, and his legs were not to be depended upon; but he managed to cover a great deal of ground, to have many painful little adventures, and to get monstrously hungry and thirsty before he happened to look in upon Penrod and Sam.

When the two boys chased him up the alley they had no intention to cause pain; they had no intention at all. They were no more cruel than Duke, Penrod's little old dog, who followed his own instincts, and, making his appearance hastily through a hole in the back fence, joined the pursuit with sound and fury. A boy will nearly always run after anything that is running, and his first impulse is to throw a stone at it. This is a survival of primeval man, who must take every chance to get his dinner. So, when Penrod and Sam drove the hapless Whitey up the alley, they were really responding to an impulse thousands and thousands of years old—an impulse founded upon the primordial observation that whatever runs is likely to prove edible. Penrod and Sam were not "bad"; they were never that. They were something which was not their fault; they were historic.

At the next corner Whitey turned to the right into the cross-street; thence, turning to the right again and still warmly pursued, he zigzagged down a main thoroughfare until he reached another cross-street, which ran alongside the Schofields' yard and brought him to the foot of the alley he had left behind in his flight. He entered the alley, and there his dim eye fell upon the open door he had previously investigated. No memory of it remained, but the place had a look associated in his mind with hay, and as Sam and Penrod turned the corner of the alley in panting yet still vociferous pursuit, Whitey stumbled up the inclined platform before the open doors, staggered thunderously across the carriage-house and through another open door into a stall, an apartment vacant since the occupancy of Mr. Schofield's last horse, now several years deceased.

CHAPTER VIII

SALVAGE

THE two boys shrieked with excitement as they beheld the coincidence of this strange return. They burst into the stable, making almost as much noise as Duke, who had become frantic at the invasion. Sam laid hands upon a rake.

"You get out o' there, you ole horse, you!" he bellowed. "I ain't afraid to drive him out. I——"

"*Wait* a minute!" shouted Penrod. "Wait till I——"

Sam was manfully preparing to enter the stall.

"You hold the doors open," he commanded, "so's they won't blow shut and keep him in here. I'm goin' to hit him with——"

"Quee-*yut !*" Penrod shouted, grasping the handle of the rake so that Sam could not use it. "Wait a *minute*, can't you?" He turned with ferocious voice and gestures upon Duke. "*Duke !*" And Duke, in spite of his excitement, was so impressed that he

109

prostrated himself in silence, and then unobtrusively withdrew from the stable. Penrod ran to the alley doors and closed them.

"My gracious!" Sam protested. "What you goin' to do?"

"I'm goin' to keep this horse," said Penrod, whose face showed the strain of a great idea.

"What *for* ?"

"For the reward," said Penrod simply.

Sam sat down in the wheelbarrow and stared at his friend almost with awe.

"My gracious," he said, "I never thought o' that! How—how much do you think we'll get, Penrod?"

Sam's thus admitting himself to a full partnership in the enterprise met no objection from Penrod, who was absorbed in the contemplation of Whitey.

"Well," he said judicially, "we might get more and we might get less."

Sam rose and joined his friend in the doorway opening upon the two stalls. Whitey had preëmpted the nearer, and was hungrily nuzzling the old frayed hollows in the manger.

"Maybe a hundred dollars—or sumpthing?" Sam asked in a low voice.

Penrod maintained his composure and repeated

the new-found expression which had sounded well to him a moment before. He recognized it as a symbol of the non-committal attitude that makes people looked up to. "Well"—he made it slow, and frowned—"we might get more and we might get less."

"More'n a hundred *dollars?*" Sam gasped.

"Well," said Penrod, "we might get more and we might get less." This time, however, he felt the need of adding something. He put a question in an indulgent tone, as though he were inquiring, not to add to his own information but to discover the extent of Sam's. "How much do you think horses are worth, anyway?"

"I don't know," said Sam frankly, and, unconsciously, he added, "They might be more and they might be less."

"Well, when our ole horse died," said Penrod, "papa said he wouldn't taken five hundred dollars for him. That's how much *horses* are worth!"

"My gracious!" Sam exclaimed. Then he had a practical afterthought. "But maybe he was a better horse than this'n. What colour was he?"

"He was bay. Looky here, Sam"—and now Penrod's manner changed from the superior to the eager—"you look what kind of horses they have in a circus, and you bet a circus has the *best* horses, don't it? Well, what kind of horses do they have in a circus? They have some black and white ones, but the best they have are white all over. Well, what kind of a horse is this we got here? He's perty near white right now, and I bet if we washed him off and got him fixed up nice he *would* be white. Well, a bay horse is worth five hundred dollars, because that's what papa said, and this horse——"

Sam interrupted rather timidly.

"He—he's awful bony, Penrod. You don't guess that'd make any——"

Penrod laughed contemptuously.

"Bony! All he needs is a little food and he'll fill right up and look good as ever. You don't know much about horses, Sam, I expect. Why, *our* ole horse——"

"Do you expect he's hungry now?" asked Sam, staring at Whitey.

"Let's try him," said Penrod. "Horses like hay and oats the best, but they'll eat most anything."

"I guess they will. He's tryin' to eat that manger up right now, and I bet it ain't good for him."

"Come on," said Penrod, closing the door that

gave entrance to the stalls. "We got to get this horse some drinkin'-water and some good food."

They tried Whitey's appetite first with an autumnal branch which they wrenched from a hardy maple in the yard. They had seen horses nibble leaves, and they expected Whitey to nibble the leaves of this branch, but his ravenous condition did not allow him time for cool discriminations. Sam poked the branch at him from the passageway, and Whitey, after one backward movement of alarm, seized it venomously.

"Here! You stop that!" Sam shouted. "You stop that, you ole horse, you!"

"What's the matter?" called Penrod from the hydrant, where he was filling a bucket. "What's he doin' now?"

"Doin'! He's eatin' the wood part, too! He's chewin' up sticks as big as baseball bats! He's crazy!"

Penrod rushed to see this sight, and stood aghast.

"Take it away from him, Sam!" he commanded sharply.

"Go on, take it away from him yourself!" was the prompt retort of his comrade.

"You had no biz'nuss to give it to him," said

Penrod. "Anybody with any sense ought to know it'd make him sick. What'd you want to go and give it to him for?"

"Well, you didn't say not to."

"Well, what if I didn't? I never said I did; did I? You go on in that stall and take it away from him."

"*Yes*, I will!" Sam returned bitterly. Then, as Whitey had dragged the remains of the branch from the manger to the floor of the stall, Sam scrambled to the top of the manger and looked over. "There ain't much left to *take* away! He's swallered it all except some splinters. Better give him the water to try and wash it down with." And, as Penrod complied, "My gracious, look at that horse *drink!*"

They gave Whitey four buckets of water, and then debated the question of nourishment. Obviously, this horse could not be trusted with branches, and, after getting their knees black and their backs sodden, they gave up trying to pull enough grass to sustain him. Then Penrod remembered that horses like apples, both "cooking-apples" and "eating-apples," and Sam mentioned the fact that every autumn his father received a barrel of "cooking-apples" from a cousin who owned a farm. That barrel was in the

Williams' cellar now, and the cellar was providentially supplied with "outside doors," so that it could be visited without going through the house. Sam and Penrod set forth for the cellar.

They returned to the stable bulging, and, after a discussion of Whitey's digestion (Sam claiming that eating the core and seeds, as Whitey did, would grow trees in his inside), they went back to the cellar for supplies again—and again. They made six trips, carrying each time a capacity cargo of apples, and still Whitey ate in a famished manner. They were afraid to take more apples from the barrel, which began to show conspicuously the result of their raids, wherefore Penrod made an unostentatious visit to the cellar of his own house. From the inside he opened a window and passed vegetables out to Sam, who placed them in a bucket and carried them hurriedly to the stable, while Penrod returned in a casual manner through the house. Of his *sang-froid* under a great strain it is sufficient to relate that, in the kitchen, he said suddenly to Della, the cook, "Oh, look behind you!" and by the time Della discovered that there was nothing unusual behind her, Penrod was gone, and a loaf of bread from the kitchen table was gone with him.

Whitey now ate nine turnips, two heads of lettuce, one cabbage, eleven raw potatoes, and the
loaf of bread. He ate the loaf of bread last and he
was a long time about it; so the boys came to a not
unreasonable conclusion.

"Well, sir, I guess we got him filled up at last!"
said Penrod. "I bet he wouldn't eat a saucer of
ice-cream now, if we'd give it to him!"

"He looks better to me," said Sam, staring criti-
cally at Whitey. "I think he's kind of begun to
fill out some. I expect he must like us, Penrod;
we been doin' a good deal for this horse."

"Well, we got to keep it up," Penrod insisted
rather pompously. "Long as *I* got charge o' this
horse, he's goin' to get good treatment."

"What we better do now, Penrod?"

Penrod took on the outward signs of deep thought.

"Well, there's plenty to *do*, all right. I got to
think."

Sam made several suggestions, which Penrod—
maintaining his air of preoccupation—dismissed
with mere gestures.

"Oh, *I* know!" Sam cried finally. "We ought
to wash him so's he'll look whiter'n what he does now.
We can turn the hose on him acrost the manger."

"No; not yet," said Penrod. "It's too soon after his meal. You ought to know that yourself. What we got to do is to make up a bed for him—if he wants to lay down or anything."

"Make up a what for him?" Sam echoed, dumfounded. "What you talkin' about? How can——"

"Sawdust," said Penrod. "That's the way the horse we used to have used to have it. We'll make this horse's bed in the other stall, and then he can go in there and lay down whenever he wants to."

"How we goin' to do it?"

"Look, Sam; there's the hole into the sawdust-box! All you got to do is walk in there with the shovel, stick the shovel in the hole till it gets full of sawdust, and then sprinkle it around on the empty stall."

"All *I* got to do!" Sam cried. "What are you goin' to do?"

"I'm goin' to be right here," Penrod answered reassuringly. "He won't kick or anything, and it isn't goin' to take you half a second to slip around behind him to the other stall."

"What makes you think he won't kick?"

"Well, I *know* he won't, and, besides, you could hit him with the shovel if he tried to. Anyhow, I'll be right here, won't I?"

"I don't care where you are," Sam said earnestly.
"What difference would that make if he ki——"

"Why, you were goin' right in the stall," Penrod
reminded him. "When he first came in, you were
goin' to take the rake and——"

"I don't care if I was," Sam declared. "I was
excited then."

"Well, you can get excited now, can't you?" his
friend urged. "You can just as easy get——"

He was interrupted by a shout from Sam, who was
keeping his eye upon Whitey throughout the discussion.

"Look! Looky there!" And undoubtedly renewing his excitement, Sam pointed at the long,
gaunt head beyond the manger. It was disappearing
from view. "Look!" Sam shouted. "He's layin'
down!"

"Well, then," said Penrod, "I guess he's goin'
to take a nap. If he wants to lay down without
waitin' for us to get the sawdust fixed for him, that's
his lookout, not ours."

On the contrary, Sam perceived a favourable opportunity for action.

"I just as soon go and make his bed up while he's
layin' down," he volunteered. "You climb up on

the manger and watch him, Penrod, and I'll sneak in
the other stall and fix it all up nice for him, so's he
can go in there any time when he wakes up, and lay
down again, or anything; and if he starts to get up,
you holler and I'll jump out over the other manger."

Accordingly, Penrod established himself in a
position to observe the recumbent figure. Whitey's
breathing was rather laboured but regular, and, as
Sam remarked, he looked "better," even in his
slumber. It is not to be doubted that, although
Whitey was suffering from a light attack of colic,
his feelings were in the main those of contentment.
After trouble, he was solaced; after exposure, he was
sheltered; after hunger and thirst, he was fed and
watered. He slept.

The noon whistles blew before Sam's task was
finished, but by the time he departed for lunch there
was made a bed of such quality that Whitey must
needs have been a born faultfinder if he complained
of it. The friends parted, each urging the other to
be prompt in returning, but Penrod got into threatening difficulties as soon as he entered the house.

CHAPTER IX

REWARD OF MERIT

P ENROD," said his mother, "what did you
do with that loaf of bread Della says you
took from the table?"

"Ma'am? *What* loaf o' bread?"

"I believe I can't let you go outdoors this afternoon," Mrs. Schofield said severely. "If you were
hungry, you know perfectly well all you had to do
was to——"

"But I wasn't hungry; I——"

"You can explain later," said Mrs. Schofield.
"You'll have all afternoon."

Penrod's heart grew cold.

"I *can't* stay in," he protested. "I've asked Sam
Williams to come over."

"I'll telephone Mrs. Williams."

"Mamma!" Penrod's voice became agonized.
"I *had* to give that bread to a——to a poor ole man.
He was starving and so were his children and his
wife. They were all just *starving*—and they couldn't

wait while I took time to come and ask you, mamma. I *got* to go outdoors this afternoon. I *got* to! Sam's——"

She relented.

In the carriage-house, half an hour later, Penrod gave an account of the episode.

"Where'd we been, I'd just like to know," he concluded, "if I hadn't got out here this afternoon?"

"Well, I guess I could managed him all right," said Sam. "I was in the passageway, a minute ago, takin' a look at him. He's standin' up again. I expect he wants more to eat."

"Well, we got to fix about that," said Penrod. "But what I mean—if I'd had to stay in the house, where would we been about the most important thing in the whole biz'nuss?"

"What you talkin' about?"

"Well, why can't you wait till I tell you?" Penrod's tone had become peevish. For that matter, so had Sam's; they were developing one of the little differences, or quarrels, that composed the very texture of their friendship.

"Well, why don't you tell me, then?"

"Well, how can I?" Penrod demanded. "You keep talkin' every minute."

"I'm not talkin' *now*, am I?" Sam protested.
"You can tell me *now*, can't you? I'm not talk——"

"You are, too!" shouted Penrod. "You talk all
the time! You——"

He was interrupted by Whitey's peculiar cough.
Both boys jumped and forgot their argument.

"He means he wants some more to eat, I bet,"
said Sam.

"Well, if he does, he's got to wait," Penrod declared. "We got to get the most important thing of
all fixed up first."

"What's that, Penrod?"

"The reward," said Penrod mildly. "That's what
I was tryin' to tell you about, Sam, if you'd ever
give me half a chance."

"Well, I *did* give you a chance. I kept *tellin'*
you to tell me, but——"

"You never! You kept sayin'——"

They renewed this discussion, protracting it in-
definitely; but as each persisted in clinging to his
own interpretation of the facts, the question still
remains unsettled. It was abandoned, or rather, it
merged into another during the later stages of the
debate, this other being concerned with which of the
debaters had the least "sense." Each made the

plain statement that if he were more deficient than
his opponent in that regard, self-destruction would
be his only refuge.   Each declared that he would
"rather die than be talked to death"; and then, as
the two approached a point bluntly recriminative,
Whitey coughed again, whereupon they were miraculously silent, and went into the passageway in a
perfectly amiable manner.

"I got to have a good look at him, for once,"
said Penrod, as he stared frowningly at Whitey.
"We got to fix up about that reward."

"I want to take a good ole look at him myself,"
said Sam.

After supplying Whitey with another bucket of
water, they returned to the carriage-house and seated
themselves thoughtfully.   In truth, they were something a shade more than thoughtful; the adventure
to which they had committed themselves was beginning to be a little overpowering. If Whitey had
been a dog, a goat, a fowl, or even a stray calf, they
would have felt equal to him; but now that the
earlier glow of their wild daring had disappeared,
vague apprehensions stirred. Their "good look"
at Whitey had not reassured them—he seemed large,
Gothic, and unusual.

Whisperings within them began to urge that for boys to undertake an enterprise connected with so huge an animal as an actual horse was perilous. Beneath the surface of their musings, dim but ominous prophecies moved; both boys began to have the feeling that, somehow, this affair was going to get beyond them and that they would be in heavy trouble before it was over—they knew not why. They knew why no more than they knew why they felt it imperative to keep the fact of Whitey's presence in the stable a secret from their respective families, but they did begin to realize that keeping a secret of that size was going to be attended with some difficulty. In brief, their sensations were becoming comparable to those of the man who stole a house.

Nevertheless, after a short period given to unspoken misgivings, they returned to the subject of the reward. The money-value of bay horses, as compared to white, was again discussed, and each announced his certainty that nothing less than "a good ole hunderd dollars" would be offered for the return of Whitey.

But immediately after so speaking they fell into another silence, due to sinking feelings. They had

FIG I

Reward.
White horse in Schofields
ally finders got him in
Schofields stable and will
let him taken away by by ~~paying~~
paying for good food he
has aten while ~~wat us~~
while ~~wat~~ waiting and
Reward of ~~$100~~ ~~$20~~
~~$15~~ ~~$5~~ $10

FIG II

FOND

Horse on Saturday moring
onwer can get him by ~~the~~ replying at
stable bhind Mr Schofield. You will have
to proov he is your horse he is whit with
kind of brown ~~sped~~ speks and worout
~~tail~~ tale he is geting good care and food
reword ~~$100~~ ~~$50~~ seventy five cents to
each one or we will keep him locked up.

spoken loudly and confidently, and yet they knew,
somehow, that such things were not to be. Ac-
cording to their knowledge, it was perfectly reasonable to suppose that they would receive this fortune, but they frightened themselves in speaking
of it; they knew that they *could* not have a hundred
dollars for their own. An oppression, as from something awful and criminal, descended upon them at
intervals.

Presently, however, they were warmed to a little
cheerfulness again by Penrod's suggestion that they
should put a notice in the paper. Neither of them
had the slightest idea how to get it there, but such
details as that were beyond the horizon; they occupied themselves with the question of what their
advertisement ought to "say." Finding that they
differed irreconcilably, Penrod went to a cache of
his in the sawdust-box and brought two pencils and
a supply of paper. He gave one of the pencils and
several sheets to Sam; then both boys bent themselves in silence to the labour of practical composition. Penrod produced the briefer paragraph. (See
Fig. I.) Sam's was more ample. (See Fig. II.)

Neither Sam nor Penrod showed any interest in
what the other had written, but both felt that some-

thing praiseworthy had been accomplished. Penrod exhaled a sigh, as of relief, and, in a manner he had observed his father use sometimes, he said:

"Thank goodness, *that's* off my mind, anyway!"

"What we goin' do next, Penrod?" Sam asked deferentially, the borrowed manner having some effect upon him.

"I don't know what *you're* goin' to do," Penrod returned, picking up the old cigarbox which had contained the paper and pencils. "*I'm* goin' to put mine in here, so's it'll come in handy when I haf to get at it."

"Well, I guess I'll keep mine there, too," said Sam. Thereupon he deposited his scribbled slip beside Penrod's in the cigarbox, and the box was solemnly returned to the secret place whence it had been taken.

"There, *that's* 'tended to!" said Sam, and, unconsciously imitating his friend's imitation, he gave forth audibly a breath of satisfaction and relief. Both boys felt that the financial side of their great affair had been conscientiously looked to, that the question of the reward was settled, and that everything was proceeding in a businesslike manner. Therefore, they were able to turn their attention to another matter.

This was the question of Whitey's next meal.
After their exploits of the morning, and the consequent imperilment of Penrod, they decided that
nothing more was to be done in apples, vegetables,
or bread; it was evident that Whitey must be fed
from the bosom of nature.

"We couldn't pull enough o' that frostbit ole grass
in the yard to feed him," Penrod said gloomily.
"We could work a week and not get enough to make
him swaller more'n about twice. All we got this
morning, he blew most of it away. He'd try to
scoop it in toward his teeth with his lip, and then
he'd haf to kind of blow out his breath, and after
that all the grass that'd be left was just some wet
pieces stickin' to the outsides of his face. Well,
and you know how he acted about that maple branch.
We can't trust him with branches."

Sam jumped up.

"*I* know!" he cried. "There's lots of leaves left
on the branches. We can give them to him."

"I just said——"

"I don't mean the branches," Sam explained.
"We'll leave the branches on the trees, but just pull
the leaves off the branches and put 'em in the bucket
and feed 'em to him out the bucket."

Penrod thought this plan worth trying, and for three-quarters of an hour the two boys were busy with the lower branches of various trees in the yard. Thus they managed to supply Whitey with a fair quantity of wet leaves, which he ate in a perfunctory way, displaying little of his earlier enthusiasm. And the work of his purveyors might have been more tedious if it had been less damp, for a boy is seldom bored by anything that involves his staying-out in the rain without protection. The drizzle had thickened; the leaves were heavy with water, and at every jerk the branches sent fat drops over the two collectors. They attained a noteworthy state of sogginess.

Finally, they were brought to the attention of the authorities indoors, and Della appeared upon the back porch.

"Musther Penrod," she called, "y'r mamma says ye'll c'm in the house this minute an' change y'r shoes an' stockin's an' everythun' else ye got on! D'ye hear me?"

Penrod, taken by surprise and unpleasantly alarmed, darted away from the tree he was depleting and ran for the stable.

"You tell her I'm dry as toast!" he shouted over his shoulder.

Della withdrew, wearing the air of a person gratuitously insulted; and a moment later she issued from the kitchen, carrying an umbrella. She opened it and walked resolutely to the stable.

"She says I'm to bring ye in the house," said Della, "an' I'm goin' to bring ye!"

Sam had joined Penrod in the carriage-house, and, with the beginnings of an unnamed terror, the two beheld this grim advance. But they did not stay for its culmination. Without a word to each other they hurriedly tiptoed up the stairs to the gloomy loft, and there they paused, listening.

They heard Della's steps upon the carriage-house floor.

"Ah, there's plenty places t'hide in," they heard her say; "but I'll show ye! She tole me to bring ye, and I'm——"

She was interrupted by a peculiar sound—loud, chilling, dismal, and unmistakably not of human origin. The boys knew it for Whitey's cough, but Della had not their experience. A smothered shriek reached their ears; there was a scurrying noise, and then, with horror, they heard Della's footsteps in the passageway that ran by Whitey's manger. Immediately there came a louder shriek, and

even in the anguish of knowing their secret discovered, they were shocked to hear distinctly the
words, "O Lard in hivvin!" in the well-known voice
of Della. She shrieked again, and they heard the
rush of her footfalls across the carriage-house floor.
Wild words came from the outer air, and the kitchen
door slammed violently. It was all over. She
had gone to "tell."

Penrod and Sam plunged down the stairs and
out of the stable. They climbed the back fence and
fled up the alley. They turned into Sam's yard,
and, without consultation, headed for the cellar
doors, nor paused till they found themselves in the
farthest, darkest, and gloomiest recess of the cellar.
There, perspiring, stricken with fear, they sank down
upon the earthen floor, with their moist backs against
the stone wall.

Thus with boys. The vague apprehensions that
had been creeping upon Penrod and Sam all afternoon had become monstrous; the unknown was
before them. How great their crime would turn
out to be (now that it was in the hands of grown
people), they did not know, but, since it concerned
a horse, it would undoubtedly be considered of
terrible dimensions.

Their plans for a reward, and all the things that had seemed both innocent and practical in the morning, now staggered their minds as manifestations of criminal folly. A new and terrible light seemed to play upon the day's exploits; they had chased a horse belonging to strangers, and it would be said that they deliberately drove him into the stable and there concealed him. They had, in truth, virtually stolen him, and they had stolen food for him. The waning light through the small window above them warned Penrod that his inroads upon the vegetables in his own cellar must soon be discovered. Della, that Nemesis, would seek them in order to prepare them for dinner, and she would find them not. But she would recall his excursion to the cellar, for she had seen him when he came up; and also the truth would be known concerning the loaf of bread. Altogether, Penrod felt that his case was worse than Sam's—until Sam offered a suggestion which roused such horrible possibilities concerning the principal item of their offense that all thought of the smaller indictments disappeared.

"Listen, Penrod," Sam quavered: "What—what if that—what if that ole horse maybe b'longed to a —policeman!" Sam's imagination was not of the

comforting kind. "What'd they—do to us, Penrod,
if it turned out he was some policeman's horse?"

Penrod was able only to shake his head. He
did not reply in words, but both boys thenceforth
considered it almost inevitable that Whitey had
belonged to a policeman, and in their sense of so
ultimate a disaster, they ceased for a time to brood
upon what their parents would probably do to them.
The penalty for stealing a policeman's horse would
be only a step short of capital, they were sure.
They would not be hanged; but vague, looming
sketches of something called the penitentiary began
to flicker before them.

It grew darker in the cellar, so that finally they
could not see each other.

"I guess they're huntin' for us by now," Sam said
huskily. "I don't—I don't like it much down here,
Penrod."

Penrod's hoarse whisper came from the profound
gloom:

"Well, who ever said you did?"

"Well——" Sam paused; then he said plaintively,
"I wish we'd never *seen* that dern ole horse."

"It was every bit his fault," said Penrod. "*We*
didn't do anything. If he hadn't come stickin' his

ole head in our stable, it'd never happened at all.
Ole fool!" He rose. "I'm goin' to get out of here;
I guess I've stood about enough for one day."

"Where—where you goin', Penrod? You aren't
goin' *home*, are you?"

"No; I'm not! What you take me for? You
think I'm crazy?"

"Well, where *can* we go?"

How far Penrod's desperation actually would have
led him is doubtful, but he made this statement:

"I don't know where *you're* goin', but *I'm* goin'
to walk straight out in the country till I come to a
farmhouse and say my name's George and live there!"

"I'll do it, too," Sam whispered eagerly. "I'll
say my name's Henry."

"Well, we better get started," said the executive
Penrod. "We got to get away from here, anyway."

But when they came to ascend the steps leading
to the "outside doors," they found that those doors
had been closed and locked for the night.

"It's no use," Sam lamented, "and we can't bust
'em, cause I tried to, once before. Fanny always
locks 'em about five o'clock—I forgot. We got to
go up the stairway and try to sneak out through the
house."

They tiptoed back, and up the inner stairs. They paused at the top, then breathlessly stepped out into a hall which was entirely dark. Sam touched Penrod's sleeve in warning, and bent to listen at a door.

Immediately that door opened, revealing the bright library, where sat Penrod's mother and Sam's father.

It was Sam's mother who had opened the door.

"Come into the library, boys," she said. "Mrs. Schofield is just telling us about it."

And as the two comrades moved dumbly into the lighted room, Penrod's mother rose, and, taking him by the shoulder, urged him close to the fire.

"You stand there and try to dry off a little, while I finish telling Mr. and Mrs. Williams about you and Sam," she said. "You'd better make Sam keep near the fire, too, Mrs. Williams, because they both got wringing wet. Think of their running off just when most people would have wanted to stay! Well, I'll go on with the story, then. Della told me all about it, and what the cook next door said *she'd* seen, how they'd been trying to pull grass and leaves for the poor old thing all day—and all about the apples they carried from *your* cellar, and getting wet and working in the rain as hard as they could

—and they'd given him a loaf of bread! Shame on you, Penrod!" She paused to laugh, but there was a little moisture round her eyes, even before she laughed. "And they'd fed him on potatoes and lettuce and cabbage and turnips out of *our* cellar! And I wish you'd see the sawdust bed they made for him! Well, when I'd telephoned, and the Humane Society man got there, he said it was the most touching thing he ever knew. It seems he *knew* this horse, and had been looking for him. He said ninety-nine boys out of a hundred would have chased the poor old thing away, and he was going to see to it that this case didn't go unnoticed, because the local branch of the society gives little silver medals for special acts like this. And the last thing he said before he led the poor old horse away was that he was sure Penrod and Sam each would be awarded one at the meeting of the society next Thursday night."

. . . On the following Saturday morning a yodel sounded from the sunny sidewalk in front of the Schofields' house, and Penrod, issuing forth, beheld the familiar figure of Samuel Williams in waiting.

Upon Sam's breast there glittered a round bit of silver suspended by a white ribbon from a bar of the same metal. Upon the breast of Penrod was a decoration precisely similar.

"'Lo, Penrod," said Sam. "What you goin' to do?"

"Nothin'."

"I got mine on," said Sam.

"I have, too," said Penrod. "I wouldn't take a hunderd dollars for mine."

"I wouldn't take two hunderd for mine," said Sam.

Each glanced pleasantly at the other's medal. They faced each other without shame. Neither had the slightest sense of hypocrisy either in himself or in his comrade. On the contrary!

Penrod's eyes went from Sam's medal back to his own; thence they wandered, with perhaps a little disappointment, to the lifeless street and to the empty yards and spectatorless windows of the neighbourhood. Then he looked southward toward the busy heart of the town, where multitudes were.

"Let's go down and see what time it is by the court-house clock," said Penrod.

CHAPTER X

MRS. SCHOFIELD had been away for three days, visiting her sister in Dayton, Illinois, and on the train, coming back, she fell into a reverie. Little dramas of memory were reënacted in her pensive mind, and through all of them moved the figure of Penrod as a principal figure, or star. These little dramas did not present Penrod as he really was, much less did they glow with the uncertain but glamorous light in which Penrod saw himself. No; Mrs. Schofield had indulged herself in absence from her family merely for her own pleasure, and now that she was homeward bound, her conscience was asserting itself; the fact that she had enjoyed her visit began to take on the aspect of a crime.

She had heard from her family only once during the three days—the message, "All well don't worry enjoy yourself," telegraphed by Mr. Schofield, and she had followed his suggestions to a reasonable extent. Of course she had worried—but only at times; wherefore she now suffered more and more poignant pangs of shame because she had not worried constantly. Naturally, the figure of Penrod, in her railway reverie, was that of an invalid.

She recalled all the illnesses of his babyhood and all those of his boyhood. She reconstructed scene after scene, with the hero always prostrate and the family physician opening the black case of phials. She emphatically renewed her recollection of accidental misfortunes to the body of Penrod Schofield, omitting neither the considerable nor the inconsiderable, forgetting no strain, sprain, cut, bruise, or dislocation of which she had knowledge. And, running this film in a sequence unrelieved by brighter interludes, she produced a biographical picture of such consistent and unremittent gloom that Penrod's past appeared to justify disturbing thoughts about his present and future.

She became less and less at ease, reproaching herself for having gone away, wondering how she had brought herself to do such a crazy thing, for it seemed to her that the members of her family were almost helpless without her guidance; they were apt to do anything—anything at all—or to catch anything.

The more she thought about her having left these
irresponsible harebrains unprotected and undirected
for three days, the less she was able to account for
her action. It seemed to her that she must have
been a little flighty, but, shaking her head grimly,
she decided that flightiness was not a good excuse.
And she made up her mind that if, upon her arrival,
she found poor little neglected Penrod and Margaret
and Mr. Schofield spared to her, safe and sound,
she would make up to them—especially to Penrod—
for all her lack of care in the past, and for this present
wild folly of spending three whole days and nights
with her sister, far away in Dayton, Illinois. Consequently, when Mrs. Schofield descended from that
train, she wore the hurried but determined expression which was always the effect upon her of a
guilty conscience.

"You're *sure* Penrod is well now?" she repeated,
after Mr. Schofield had seated himself at her side
in a vehicle known to its driver as a "deepoe
hack."

"'Well *now?*'" he said. "He's been well all the
time. I've told you twice that he's all right."

"Men can't always see." She shook her head
impatiently. "I haven't been a bit sure he was well

lately. I don't think he's been really well for two or three months. How has he seemed to-day?"

"In fair health," Mr. Schofield replied thoughtfully. "Della called me up at the office to tell me that one of the telephone trouble-men had come into the house to say that if that durn boy didn't quit climbing their poles they'd have him arrested. They said he——"

"That's it!" Mrs. Schofield interrupted quickly. "He's nervous. It's some nervous trouble makes him act like that. He's not like himself at all."

"Sometimes," said Mr. Schofield, "I wish he weren't."

"When he's himself," Mrs. Schofield went on anxiously, "he's very quiet and good; he doesn't go climbing telegraph-poles and reckless things like that. And I noticed before I went away that he was growing twitchy, and seemed to be getting the habit of making unpleasant little noises in his throat."

"Don't fret about that," said her husband. "He was trying to learn Sam Williams's imitation of a bullfrog's croak. I used to do that myself when I was a boy. Gl-glump, gallump! No; I can't do it now. But nearly all boys feel obliged to learn it."

"You're entirely mistaken, Henry," she returned

a little sharply. "That isn't the way he goes in his throat. Penrod is getting to be a *very* nervous boy, and he makes noises because he can't help it. He works part of his face, too, sometimes, so much that I've been afraid it would interfere with his looks."

"Interfere with his what?" For the moment, Mr. Schofield seemed to be dazed.

"When he's himself," she returned crisply, "he's quite a handsome boy."

"He is?"

"Handsomer than the average, anyhow," said Mrs. Schofield firmly. "No wonder you don't see it— when we've let his system get all run down like this!"

"Good heavens!" murmured the mystified Mr. Schofield. "Penrod's system hasn't been running down; its just the same as it always was. He's absolutely all right."

"Indeed he is not!" she said severely. "We've got to take better care of him than we have been."

"Why, how could——"

"I know what I'm talking about," she interrupted. "Penrod is anything but a strong boy, and it's all our fault. We haven't been watchful enough of his health; that's what's the matter with him and makes him so nervous."

Thus she continued, and, as she talked on, Mr. Schofield began, by imperceptible processes, to adopt her views. As for Mrs. Schofield herself, these views became substantial by becoming vocal. This is to say, with all deference, that, as soon-as she heard herself stating them she was convinced that they accurately represented facts. And the determined look in her eyes deepened when the "deepoe hack" turned the familiar corner and she saw Penrod running to the gate, followed by his little old dog, Duke.

Never had Penrod been so glad to greet his mother. Never was he more boisterous in the expression of happiness of that kind. And the tokens of his appetite at dinner, a little later, were extraordinary. Mr. Schofield began to feel reassured in spite of himself, but Mrs. Schofield shook her head.

"Don't you see? It's abnormal!" she said, in a low, decisive voice.

That night Penrod awoke from a sweet, conscienceless slumber—or, rather, he was awakened. A wrappered form lurked over him in the gloom.

"Uff—ow——" he muttered, and turned his face from the dim light that shone through the doorway. He sighed and sought the depths of sleep again.

"Penrod," said his mother softly, and, while he resisted feebly, she turned him over to face her.

"Gawn lea' me 'lone," he muttered.

Then, as a little sphere touched his lips, he jerked his head away, startled.

"Whassat?"

Mrs. Schofield replied in tones honeysweet and coaxing:

"It's just a nice little pill, Penrod."

"Doe waw 'ny!" he protested, keeping his eyes shut, clinging to the sleep from which he was being riven.

"Be a good boy, Penrod," she whispered. "Here's a glass of nice cool water to swallow it down with. Come, dear; it's going to do you lots of good."

And again the little pill was placed suggestively against his lips; but his head jerked backward, and his hand struck out in blind, instinctive self-defense.

"I'll *bust* that ole pill," he muttered, still with closed eyes. "Lemme get my han's on it an' I will!"

"Penrod!"

"*Please* go on away, mamma!"

"I will, just as soon as you take this little pill."

"I *did*."

"No, dear."

"I did," Penrod insisted plaintively. "You made me take it just before I went to bed."

"Oh, yes; *that* one. But, dearie," Mrs. Schofield explained, "I got to thinking about it after I went to bed, and I decided you'd better have another." - - -

"I don't *want* another."

"Yes, dearie."

"Please go 'way and let me sleep."

"Not till you've taken the little pill, dear."

"Oh, *golly !*" Groaning, he propped himself upon an elbow and allowed the pill to pass between his lips. (He would have allowed anything whatever to pass between them, if that passing permitted his return to slumber.) Then, detaining the pill in his mouth, he swallowed half a glass of water, and again was recumbent.

"G'-night, mamma."

"Good-night, dearie. Sleep well."

"Yes'm."

After her departure Penrod drowsily enjoyed the sugar coating of the pill, but this was indeed a brief pleasure. A bitterness that was like a pang suddenly made itself known to his sense of taste, and he realized that he had dallied too confidingly with the product of a manufacturing chemist who should have been indicted for criminal economy. The medicinal portion of the little pill struck the wall with a faint tap, then dropped noiselessly to the floor, and, after a time, Penrod slept.

Some hours later he began to dream; he dreamed that his feet and legs were becoming uncomfortable as a result of Sam Williams' activities with a red-hot poker.

"You *quit* that!" he said aloud, and awoke indignantly. Again a dark, wrappered figure hovered over the bed.

"It's only a hot-water bag, dear," said Mrs. Schofield, still labouring under the covers with an extended arm. "You mustn't hunch yourself up that way, Penrod. Put your feet down on it."

And, as he continued to hunch himself, she moved the bag in the direction of his withdrawal.

"Ow, murder!" he exclaimed convulsively. "What you tryin' to do? Scald me to death?"

"Penrod——"

"My goodness, mamma," he wailed; "can't you let me sleep a *minute*?"

"It's very bad for you to let your feet get cold, dear."

"They *weren't* cold. I don't want any ole hot-wat——"

"Penrod," she said firmly, "you must put your feet against the bag. It isn't too hot."

"Oh, isn't it?" he retorted. "I don't s'pose you'd care if I burned my feet right off! Mamma, won't you please, pul-*leeze* let me get some sleep?"

"Not till you——"

She was interrupted by a groan which seemed to come from an abyss.

"All right, I'll do it! Let 'em burn, then!" Thus spake the desperate Penrod; and Mrs. Schofield was able to ascertain that one heel had been placed in light contact with the bag.

"No; both feet, Penrod."

With a tragic shiver he obeyed.

"*That's* right, dear! Now, keep them that way. It's good for you. Good-night."

"G'-night!"

The door closed softly behind her, and the body of Penrod, from the hips upward, rose invisibly in the complete darkness of the bedchamber. A moment later the hot-water bag reached the floor in as noiseless a manner as that previously adopted by the remains of the little pill, and Penrod once more bespread his soul with poppies. This time he slept until the breakfast-bell rang.

He was late to school, and at once found himself in difficulties. Government demanded an explanation of the tardiness, but Penrod made no reply of any kind. Taciturnity is seldom more strikingly out of place than under such circumstances, and the penalties imposed took account not only of Penrod's tardiness but of his supposititious defiance of authority in declining to speak. The truth was that Penrod did not know why he was tardy, and, with mind still lethargic, found it impossible to think of an excuse —his continuing silence being due merely to the persistence of his efforts to invent one. Thus were his meek searchings misinterpreted, and the unloved hours of improvement in science and the arts made odious.

"They'll *see !*" he whispered sorely to himself, as he bent low over his desk, a little later. Some day he would "show 'em." The picture in his mind was of a vast, vague assembly of people headed by Miss Spence and the superior pupils who were never tardy, and these multitudes, representing persecution and government in general, were all cringing before a Penrod Schofield who rode a grim black horse up and down their miserable ranks, and gave curt orders.

"Make 'em step back there!" he commanded his myrmidons savagely. "Fix it so's your horses'll step on their feet if they don't do what I say!" Then, from his shining saddle, he watched the throngs slinking away. "I guess they know who I am *now!*"

CHAPTER XI

THE TONIC

THESE broodings helped a little, but it was a severe morning, and on his way home at noon he did not recover heart enough to practise the bullfrog's croak, the craft of which Sam Williams had lately mastered to inspiring perfection. This sonorous accomplishment Penrod had determined to make his own. At once guttural and resonant, impudent yet plaintive, with a barbaric twang like the plucked string of a Congo war-fiddle, the sound had fascinated him. It is made in the throat by processes utterly impossible to describe in human words, and no alphabet as yet produced by civilized man affords the symbols to vocalize it to the ear of imagination. "Gunk" is the poor makeshift which must be employed to indicate it.

Penrod uttered one half-hearted "*Gunk*" as he turned in at his own gate. However, this stimulated him, and he paused to practise. "*Gunk!*" he croaked. "*Gunk—gunk—gunk—gunk!*"

149

Mrs. Schofield leaned out of an open window up-stairs.

"Don't do that, Penrod," she said anxiously. "Please don't do that."

"Why not?" asked Penrod, and feeling encouraged by his progress in the new art, he continued: "*Gunk! Gunk—gunk—gunk! Gunk—gunk——*"

"Please try not to do it," she urged pleadingly. "You *can* stop it if you try. Won't you, dear?"

But Penrod felt that he was almost upon the point of attaining a mastery equal to that of Sam Williams. He had just managed to do something in his throat that he had never done before, and he felt that unless he kept on doing it at this time, his new-born facility might evade him later. "*Gunk!*" he croaked. "*Gunk—gunk—gunk!*"   And he continued to croak, persevering monotonously, his expression indicating the depth of his preoccupation.

His mother looked down solicitously, murmured in a melancholy undertone, shook her head; then disappeared from the window, and, after a moment or two, opened the front door.

"Come in, dear," she said; "I've got something for you."

Penrod's look of preoccupation vanished; he

brightened and ceased to croak. His mother had already given him a small leather pocketbook with a nickel in it, as a souvenir of her journey. Evidently she had brought another gift as well, delaying its presentation until now. "I've got something for you!" These were auspicious words.

"What is it, mamma?" he asked, and as she smiled tenderly upon him, his gayety increased. "Yay!" he shouted. "Mamma, is it that reg'lar carpenter's tool chest I told you about?"

"No," she said. "But I'll show you, Penrod. Come on, dear."

He followed her with alacrity to the dining-room, and the bright anticipation in his eyes grew more brilliant—until she opened the door of the china-closet, simultaneously with that action announcing cheerily:

"It's something that's going to do you lots of good, Penrod."

He was instantly chilled, for experience had taught him that when predictions of this character were made, nothing pleasant need be expected. Two seconds later his last hope departed as she turned from the closet and he beheld in her hands a quart bottle containing what appeared to be a section of grassy swamp immersed in a cloudy brown liquor. He stepped back, grave suspicion in his glance.

"What *is* that?" he asked, in a hard voice.

Mrs. Schofield smiled upon him.

"It's nothing," she said. "That is, it's nothing you'll mind at all. It's just so you won't be so nervous."

"I'm not nervous."

"You don't think so, of course, dear," she returned, and, as she spoke, she poured some of the brown liquor into a tablespoon. "People often can't tell when they're nervous themselves; but your papa and I have been getting a little anxious about you, dear, and so I got this medicine for you."

"*Where'd* you get it?" he demanded.

Mrs. Schofield set the bottle down and moved toward him, insinuatingly extending the full tablespoon.

"Here, dear," she said; "just take this little spoonful, like a goo——"

"I want to know where it came from," he insisted darkly, again stepping backward.

"Where?" she echoed absently, watching to see that nothing was spilled from the spoon as she con-

tinued to move toward him. "Why, I was talking
to old Mrs. Wottaw at market this morning, and
she said her son Clark used to have nervous trouble,
and she told me about this medicine and how to
have it made at the drug store. She told me it
cured Clark, and——"

"I don't want to be cured," said Penrod, adding
inconsistently, "I haven't got anything to be cured
of."

"Now, dear," Mrs. Schofield began, "you don't
want your papa and me to keep on worrying
about——"

"I don't care whether you worry or not," the heart-
less boy interrupted. "I don't want to take any
horrable ole medicine. What's that grass and weeds
in the bottle for?"

Mrs. Schofield looked grieved.

"There isn't any grass and there aren't any weeds;
those are healthful herbs."

"I bet they'll make me sick."

She sighed.

"Penrod, we're trying to make you well."

"But I *am* well, I tell you!"

"No, dear; your papa's been very much troubled
about you. Come, Penrod; swallow this down and

don't make such a fuss about it. It's just for your own good."

And she advanced upon him again, the spoon extended toward his lips. It almost touched them for he had retreated until his back was against the wall-paper. He could go no farther, but he evinced his unshaken repugnance by averting his face.

"What's it taste like?" he demanded.

"It's not unpleasant at all," she answered, poking the spoon at his mouth. "Mrs. Wottaw said Clark used to be very fond of it. 'It doesn't taste like ordinary medicine at all,' she said."

"How often I got to take it?" Penrod mumbled, as the persistent spoon sought to enter his mouth. "Just this once?"

"No, dear; three times a day."

"I won't do it!"

"Penrod!" She spoke sharply. "You swallow this down and stop making such a fuss. I can't be all day. Hurry!"

She inserted the spoon between his lips, so that its rim touched his clenched teeth; he was still reluctant. Moreover, his reluctance was natural and characteristic, for a boy's sense of taste is as simple

"Penrod did not reply. His expression had become peculiar, and the peculiarity of his manner was equal to that of his expression"

and as peculiar as a dog's though, of course, altogether different from a dog's. A boy, passing through the experimental age, may eat and drink astonishing things, but they must be of his own choosing. His palate is tender, and, in one sense, might be called fastidious; nothing is more sensitive or more easily shocked. A boy tastes things much *more* than grown people taste them: what is merely unpleasant to a man is sheer broth of hell to a boy. Therefore, not knowing what might be encountered, Penrod continued to be reluctant.

"Penrod," his mother exclaimed, losing patience, "I'll call your papa, to make you take it, if you don't swallow it right down! Open your mouth, Penrod! It isn't going to taste bad at all. Open your mouth —*there !*"

The reluctant jaw relaxed at last, and Mrs. Schofield dexterously elevated the handle of the spoon so that the brown liquor was deposited within her son.

"There!" she repeated triumphantly. "It wasn't so bad after all, was it?"

Penrod did not reply. His expression had become odd, and the oddity of his manner was equal to that of his expression. Uttering no sound, he seemed to distend, as if he had suddenly become a pneumatic boy under dangerous pressure. Meanwhile, his reddening eyes, fixed awfully upon his mother, grew unbearable.

"Now, it wasn't such a bad taste," said Mrs. Schofield rather nervously. "Don't go acting *that* way, Penrod!"

But Penrod could not help himself. In truth, even a grown person hardened to all manner of flavours, and able to eat caviar or liquid Camembert, would have found the cloudy brown liquor virulently repulsive. It contained in solution, with other things, the vital element of surprise, for it was comparatively odourless, and, unlike the chivalrous rattlesnake, gave no warning of what it was about to do. In the case of Penrod, the surprise was complete and its effect visibly shocking.

The distention by which he began to express his emotion appeared to be increasing; his slender throat swelled as his cheeks puffed. His shoulders rose toward his ears; he lifted his right leg in an unnatural way and held it rigidly in the air.

"Stop that, Penrod!" Mrs. Schofield commanded. "You stop it!"

He found his voice.

"Uff! *Oooff!*" he said thickly, and collapsed—a mere, ordinary, every-day convulsion taking the place of his pneumatic symptoms. He began to writhe, at the same time opening and closing his mouth rapidly and repeatedly, waving his arms, stamping on the floor.

"Ow! Ow-ow-*ow!*" he vociferated.

Reassured by these normal demonstrations, of a type with which she was familiar, Mrs. Schofield resumed her fond smile.

"*You're* all right, little boysie!" she said heartily. Then, picking up the bottle, she replenished the tablespoon, and told Penrod something she had considered it undiplomatic to mention before.

"Here's the other one," she said sweetly.

"Uuf!" he sputtered. "Other—uh—what?"

"Two tablespoons before each meal," she informed him.

Instantly Penrod made the first of a series of passionate efforts to leave the room. His determination was so intense, and the manifestations of it were so ruthless, that Mrs. Schofield, exhausted, found herself obliged to call for the official head of the house—in fact, she found herself obliged to

shriek for him; and Mr. Schofield, upon hastily
entering the room, beheld his wife apparently in the
act of sawing his son back and forth across the sill
of an open window.

Penrod made a frantic effort to reach the good
green earth, even after his mother's clutch upon his
ankle had been reënforced by his father's. Nor was
the lad's revolt subdued when he was deposited upon
the floor and the window closed. Indeed, it may
be said that he actually never gave up, though it is
a fact that the second potion was successfully placed
inside him. But by the time this feat was finally
accomplished, Mr. Schofield had proved that, in
spite of middle age, he was entitled to substantial
claims and honours both as athlete and orator—his
oratory being founded less upon the school of Web-
ster and more upon that of Jeremiah.

So the thing was done, and the double dose put
within the person of Penrod Schofield. It proved
not ineffective there, and presently, as its new owner
sat morosely at table, he began to feel slightly dizzy
and his eyes refused him perfect service. This was
natural, because two tablespoons of the cloudy
brown liquor contained about the amount of alcohol
to be found in an ordinary cocktail. Now a boy

does not enjoy the effects of intoxication; enjoyment of that kind is obtained only by studious application. Therefore, Penrod spoke of his symptoms complainingly, and even showed himself so vindictive as to attribute them to the new medicine.

His mother made no reply. Instead, she nodded her head as if some inner conviction had proven well founded.

"*Bilious, too,*" she whispered to her husband.

That evening, during the half-hour preceding dinner, the dining-room was the scene of another struggle, only a little less desperate than that which had been the prelude to lunch, and again an appeal to the head of the house was found necessary. Muscular activity and a liberal imitation of the jeremiads once more subjugated the rebel—and the same rebellion and its suppression in a like manner took place the following morning before breakfast. But this was Saturday, and, without warning or apparent reason, a remarkable change came about at noon. However, Mr. and Mrs. Schofield were used to inexplicable changes in Penrod, and they missed its significance.

When Mrs. Schofield, with dread in her heart, called Penrod into the house "to take his medicine" before lunch, he came briskly, and took it like a lamb!

"Why, Penrod, that's splendid!" she cried. "You see it isn't bad, at all."

"No'm," he said meekly. "Not when you-get used to it."

"And aren't you ashamed, making all that fuss?" she went on happily.

"Yes'm, I guess so."

"And don't you feel better? Don't you see how much good it's doing you already?"

"Yes'm, I guess so."

Upon a holiday morning, several weeks later, Penrod and Sam Williams revived a pastime which they called "drug store," setting up display counters, selling chemical, cosmetic, and other compounds to imaginary customers, filling prescriptions, and variously conducting themselves in a pharmaceutical manner. They were in the midst of affairs when Penrod interrupted his partner and himself with a cry of recollection.

"*I* know!" he shouted. "I got some mighty good ole stuff we want. You wait!" And, dashing to the house, he disappeared.

Returning immediately, Penrod placed upon the principal counter of the "drug store" a large bottle. It was a quart bottle, in fact; and it contained what appeared to be a section of grassy swamp immersed in a cloudy brown liquor.

"There!" Penrod exclaimed. "How's that for some good ole medicine?"

"It's good ole stuff," Sam said approvingly. "Where'd you get it? Whose is it, Penrod?"

"It *was* mine," said Penrod. "Up to about serreval days ago, it was. They quit givin' it to me. I had to take two bottles and a half of it."

"What did you haf to take it for?"

"I got nervous, or sumpthing," said Penrod.

"You all well again now?"

"I guess so. Uncle Passloe and cousin Ronald came to visit, and I expect she was too busy to think about it, or sumpthing. Anyway, she quit makin' me take it, and said I was lots better. She's forgot all about it by this time."

Sam was looking at the bottle with great interest.

"What's all that stuff in there, Penrod?" he asked. "What's all that stuff in there looks like grass?"

"It *is* grass," said Penrod.

"How'd it get·there?"

"I stuck it in there," the candid boy replied. "First they had some horrable ole stuff in there like to killed me. But after they got three doses down me, I took the bottle out in the yard and cleaned her all out and pulled a lot o' good ole grass and stuffed her pretty full and poured in a lot of good ole hydrant water on top of it. Then, when they got the next bottle, I did the same way, and——"

"It don't look like water," Sam objected.

Penrod laughed a superior laugh.

"Oh, that's nothin'," he said, with the slight swagger of young and conscious genius. "Of course, I had to slip in and shake her up sometimes, so's they wouldn't notice."

"But what did you put in it to make it look like that?"

Penrod, upon the point of replying, happened to glance toward the house. His gaze, lifting, rested for a moment upon a window. The head of Mrs. Schofield was framed in that window. She nodded gayly to her son. She could see him plainly, and she thought that he seemed perfectly healthy, and as happy as a boy could be. She was right.

"What *did* you put in it?" Sam insisted.

And probably it was just as well that, though Mrs. Schofield could see her son, the distance was too great for her to hear him.

"Oh, nothin'," Penrod replied. "Nothin' but a little good ole mud."

CHAPTER XII

GIPSY

ON A fair Saturday afternoon in November Penrod's little old dog Duke returned to the ways of his youth and had trouble with a strange cat on the back porch. This indiscretion, so uncharacteristic, was due to the agitation of a surprised moment, for Duke's experience had inclined him to a peaceful pessimism, and he had no ambition for hazardous undertakings of any sort. He was given to musing but not to avoidable action, and he seemed habitually to hope for something which he was pretty sure would not happen. Even in his sleep, this gave him an air of wistfulness.

Thus, being asleep in a nook behind the metal refuse-can, when the strange cat ventured to ascend the steps of the porch, his appearance was so unwarlike that the cat felt encouraged to extend its field of reconnaissance—for the cook had been careless, and the backbone of a three-pound whitefish lay at the foot of the refuse-can.

164

This cat was, for a cat, needlessly tall, powerful, independent, and masculine. Once, long ago, he had been a roly-poly pepper-and-salt kitten; he had a home in those days, and a name, "Gipsy," which he abundantly justified. He was precocious in dissipation. Long before his adolescence, his lack of domesticity was ominous, and he had formed bad companionships. Meanwhile, he grew so rangy, and developed such length and power of leg and such traits of character, that the father of the little girl who owned him was almost convincing when he declared that the young cat was half broncho and half Malay pirate—though, in the light of Gipsy's later career, this seems bitterly unfair to even the lowest orders of bronchos and Malay pirates.

No; Gipsy was not the pet for a little girl. The rosy hearthstone and sheltered rug were too circumspect for him. Surrounded by the comforts of middle-class respectability, and profoundly oppressed, even in his youth, by the Puritan ideals of the household, he sometimes experienced a sense of suffocation. He wanted free air and he wanted free life; he wanted the lights, the lights, and the music. He abandoned the *bourgeoisie* irrevocably. He went forth in a

May twilight, carrying the evening beefsteak with him, and joined the underworld.

His extraordinary size, his daring, and his utter lack of sympathy soon made him the leader—and, at the same time, the terror—of all the loose-lived cats in a wide neighbourhood. He contracted no friendships and had no confidants. He seldom slept in the same place twice in succession, and though he was wanted by the police, he was not found. In appearance he did not lack distinction of an ominous sort; the slow, rhythmic, perfectly controlled mechanism of his tail, as he impressively walked abroad, was incomparably sinister. This stately and dangerous walk of his, his long, vibrant whiskers, his scars, his yellow eye, so ice-cold, so fire-hot, haughty as the eye of Satan, gave him the deadly air of a mousquetaire duellist. His soul was in that walk and in that eye; it could be read—the soul of a bravo of fortune, living on his wits and his valour, asking no favours and granting no quarter. Intolerant, proud, sullen, yet watchful and constantly planning —purely a militarist, believing in slaughter as in a religion, and confident that art, science, poetry, and the good of the world were happily advanced thereby— Gipsy had become, though technically not a wildcat, undoubtedly the most untamed cat at large in the civilized world. Such, in brief, was the terrifying creature which now elongated its neck, and, over the top step of the porch, bent a calculating scrutiny upon the wistful and slumberous Duke.

The scrutiny was searching but not prolonged. Gipsy muttered contemptuously to himself, "Oh, sheol; I'm not afraid o' *that!*" And he approached the fishbone, his padded feet making no noise upon the boards. It was a desirable fishbone, large, with a considerable portion of the fish's tail still attached to it.

It was about a foot from Duke's nose, and the little dog's dreams began to be troubled by his olfactory nerve. This faithful sentinel, on guard even while Duke slept, signalled that alarums and excursions by parties unknown were taking place, and suggested that attention might well be paid. Duke opened one drowsy eye. What that eye beheld was monstrous.

Here was a strange experience—the horrific vision in the midst of things so accustomed. Sunshine fell sweetly upon porch and backyard; yonder was the familiar stable, and from its interior came the busy hum of a carpenter shop, established that

morning by Duke's young master, in association
with Samuel Williams and Herman. Here, close
by, were the quiet refuse-can and the wonted
brooms and mops leaning against the latticed wall
at the end of the porch, and there, by the foot of the
steps, was the stone slab of the cistern, with the iron
cover displaced and lying beside the round opening, where the carpenters had left it, not half an
hour ago, after lowering a stick of wood into the
water, "to season it." All about Duke were these
usual and reassuring environs of his daily life, and
yet it was his fate to behold, right in the midst of
them, and in ghastly juxtaposition to his face, a
thing of nightmare and lunacy.

Gipsy had seized the fishbone by the middle.
Out from one side of his head, and mingling with his
whiskers, projected the long, spiked spine of the big
fish; down from the other side of that ferocious head
dangled the fish's tail, and from above the remarkable effect thus produced shot the intolerable glare
of two yellow eyes. To the gaze of Duke, still
blurred by slumber, this monstrosity was all of one
piece—the bone seemed a living part of it. What
he saw was like those interesting insect-faces which
the magnifying glass reveals to great M. Fabre.

It was impossible for Duke to maintain the philosophic calm of M. Fabre, however; there was no
magnifying glass between him and this spined and
spiky face. Indeed, Duke was not in a position to
think the matter over quietly. If he had been able to
do that, he would have said to himself: "We have here
an animal of most peculiar and unattractive appearance, though, upon examination, it seems to be only
a cat stealing a fishbone. Nevertheless, as the thief
is large beyond all my recollection of cats and has an
unpleasant stare, I will leave this spot at once."

On the contrary, Duke was so electrified by his
horrid awakening that he completely lost his presence of mind. In the very instant of his first eye's
opening, the other eye and his mouth behaved similarly, the latter loosing upon the quiet air one shriek
of mental agony before the little dog scrambled to his
feet and gave further employment to his voice in a
frenzy of profanity. At the same time the subterranean diapason of a demoniac bass viol was heard; it
rose to a wail, and rose and rose again till it screamed
like a small siren. It was Gipsy's war-cry, and,
at the sound of it, Duke became a frothing maniac.
He made a convulsive frontal attack upon the hob-
goblin—and the massacre began.

Never releasing the fishbone for an instant, Gipsy laid back his ears in a chilling way, beginning to shrink into himself like a concertina, but rising amidships so high that he appeared to be giving an imitation of that peaceful beast, the dromedary. Such was not his purpose, however, for, having attained his greatest possible altitude, he partially sat down and elevated his right arm after the manner of a semaphore. This semaphore arm remained rigid for a second, threatening; then it vibrated with inconceivable rapidity, feinting. But it was the treacherous left that did the work. Seemingly this left gave Duke three lightning little pats upon the right ear, but the change in his voice indicated that these were no love-taps. He yelled "help!" and "bloody murder!"

Never had such a shattering uproar, all vocal, broken out upon a peaceful afternoon. Gipsy possessed a vocabulary for cat-swearing certainly second to none out of Italy, and probably equal to the best there, while Duke remembered and uttered things he had not thought of for years.

The hum of the carpenter shop ceased, and Sam Williams appeared in the stable doorway. He stared insanely.

"My gorry!" he shouted. "Duke's havin' a
fight with the biggest cat you ever saw in your life!
C'mon!"

His feet were already in motion toward the battle-
field, with Penrod and Herman hurrying in his wake.
Onward they sped, and Duke was encouraged by the
sight and sound of these reënforcements to increase
his own outrageous clamours and to press home his
attack. But he was ill-advised. This time it was
the right arm of the semaphore that dipped—and
Duke's honest nose was but too conscious of what
happened in consequence.

A lump of dirt struck the refuse-can with violence,
and Gipsy beheld the advance of overwhelming
forces. They rushed upon him from two directions,
cutting off the steps of the porch. Undaunted, the
formidable cat raked Duke's nose again, somewhat
more lingeringly, and prepared to depart with his
fishbone. He had little fear for himself, because he
was inclined to think that, unhampered, he could
whip anything on earth; still, things seemed to be
growing rather warm and he saw nothing to prevent
his leaving.

And though he could laugh in the face of so un-
equal an antagonist as Duke, Gipsy felt that he

was never at his best or able to do himself full justice
unless he could perform that feline operation in-
accurately known as "spitting." To his notion,
this was an absolute essential to combat; but, as all
cats of the slightest pretensions to technique perfectly understand, it can neither be well done nor
produce the best effects unless the mouth be opened
to its utmost capacity so as to expose the beginnings
of the alimentary canal, down which—at least that
is the intention of the threat—the opposing party
will soon be passing. And Gipsy could not open
his mouth without relinquishing his fishbone.

Therefore, on small accounts he decided to leave the
field to his enemies and to carry the fishbone elsewhere.
He took two giant leaps. The first landed him upon
the edge of the porch. There, without an instant's
pause, he gathered his fur-sheathed muscles, con-
centrated himself into one big steel spring, and
launched himself superbly into space. He made a
stirring picture, however brief, as he left the solid
porch behind him and sailed upward on an ascend-
ing curve into the sunlit air. His head was proudly
up; he was the incarnation of menacing power and
of self-confidence. It is possible that the whitefish's spinal column and flopping tail had interfered

with his vision, and in launching himself he may have mistaken the dark, round opening of the cistern for its dark, round cover. In that case, it was a leap calculated and executed with precision, for as the boys clamoured their pleased astonishment, Gipsy descended accurately into the orifice and passed majestically from public view, with the fishbone still in his mouth and his haughty head still high.

There was a grand splash!

CHAPTER XIII

CONCERNING TROUSERS

DUKE, hastening to place himself upon the stone slab, raged at his enemy in safety; and presently the indomitable Gipsy could be heard from the darkness below, turning on the bass of his siren, threatening the water which enveloped him, returning Duke's profanity with interest, and cursing the general universe.

"You hush!" Penrod stormed, rushing at Duke. "You go 'way from here! You *Duke !*"

And Duke, after prostrating himself, decided that it would be a relief to obey and to consider his responsibilities in this matter at an end. He withdrew beyond a corner of the house, thinking deeply.

"Why'n't you let him bark at the ole cat?" Sam Williams inquired, sympathizing with the oppressed. "I guess you'd want to bark if a cat had been treatin' you the way this one did Duke."

"Well, we got to get this cat out o' here, haven't we?" Penrod demanded crossly.

"What fer?" asked Herman. "Mighty mean cat! If it was me, I let 'at ole cat drownd."

"My goodness!" Penrod cried. "What you want to let it drown for? Anyways, we got to use this water in our house, haven't we? You don't s'pose people like to use water that's got a cat drowned in it, do you? It gets pumped up into the tank in the attic and goes all over the house, and I bet you wouldn't want to see your father and mother usin' water a cat was drowned in. I guess I don't want my father and moth——"

"Well, how *can* we get it out?" Sam asked, cutting short this virtuous oration. "It's swimmin' around down there," he continued, peering into the cistern, "and kind of roaring, and it must of dropped its fishbone, 'cause it's spittin' just awful. I guess maybe it's mad 'cause it fell in there."

"I don't know how it's goin' to be got out," said Penrod, "but I know it's *got* to be got out, and that's all there is to it! I'm not goin' to have my father and mother——"

"Well, once," said Sam, "once when a kitten fell down *our* cistern, papa took a pair of his trousers, and he held 'em by the end of one leg, and let 'em hang down through the hole till the end of the other leg was in the water, and the kitten went and clawed hold of it, and he pulled it right up, easy as anything. Well, that's the way to do now, 'cause if a kitten could keep hold of a pair of trousers, I guess this ole cat could. It's the biggest cat *I* ever saw!—All you got to do is to go and ast your mother for a pair of your father's trousers, and we'll have this ole cat out o' there in no time."

Penrod glanced toward the house perplexedly.

"She ain't home, and I'd be afraid to——"

"Well, take your own, then," Sam suggested briskly. "You take 'em off in the stable, and wait in there, and I and Herman'll get the cat out."

Penrod had no enthusiasm for this plan, but he affected to consider it.

"Well, I don't know 'bout that," he said, and then, after gazing attentively into the cistern and making some eye measurements of his knickerbockers, he shook his head. "They'd be too short. They wouldn't be *near* long enough!"

"Then neither would mine," said Sam promptly.

"Herman's would," said Penrod.

"No, suh!" Herman had recently been promoted to long trousers, and he expressed a strong disinclination to fall in with Penrod's idea. "My mammy

sit up late nights sewin' on 'ese britches fer me,
makin' 'em outen of a pair o 'pappy's, an' they mighty
good britches.   Ain' goin' have no wet cat climbin'
up 'em!   No, suh!"

Both boys began to walk toward him argumenta-
tively, while he moved slowly backward, shaking his
head and denying them.

"I don't keer how much you talk!" he said.
"Mammy give my *ole* britches to Verman, an' 'ese
here ones on'y britches I got now, an' I'm go' to
keep 'em on me—not take 'em off an' let ole wet
cat splosh all over 'em.   My mammy, she sewed
'em fer *me*, I reckon—din' sew 'em fer no cat!"

"Oh, *please*, come on, Herman!" Penrod begged
pathetically.   "You don't want to see the poor cat
drown, do you?"

"Mighty mean cat!" said Herman.   "Bet' let
'at ole pussy-cat 'lone whur it is."

"Why, it'll only take a minute," Sam urged.
"You just wait inside the stable and you'll have
'em back on again before you could say 'Jack
Robinson.'"

"I ain' got no use to say no Jack Robason," said
Herman.   "An' I ain' go' to han' over my britches
fer *no* cat!"

"Listen here, Herman," Penrod began pleadingly. "You can watch us every minute through the crack in the stable door, can't you? We ain't goin' to *hurt* 'em any, are we? You can see everything we do, can't you? Look at here, Herman: you know that little saw you said you wished it was yours, in the carpenter shop? Well, honest, if you'll just let us take your trousers till we get this poor ole cat out the cistern, I'll give you that little saw."

Herman was shaken; he yearned for the little saw.

"You gimme her to keep?" he asked cautiously. "You gimme her befo' I han' over my britches?"

"You'll see!" Penrod ran into the stable, came back with the little saw, and placed it in Herman's hand. Herman could resist no longer, and two minutes later he stood in the necessary négligée within the shelter of the stable door, and watched, through the crack, the lowering of the surrendered garment into the cistern. His gaze was anxious, and surely nothing could have been more natural, since the removal had exposed Herman's brown legs, and although the weather was far from inclement, November is never quite the month for people to be out of doors entirely without leg-covering. Therefore, he marked with impatience that Sam and

Penrod, after lowering the trousers partway to the water, had withdrawn them and fallen into an argument.

"Name o' goo'ness!" Herman shouted. "I ain' got no time fer you all do so much talkin'. If you go' git 'at cat out, why'n't you *git* him?"

"Wait just a minute," Penrod called, and he came running to the stable, seized upon a large wooden box, which the carpenters had fitted with a lid and leather hinges, and returned with it cumbersomely to the cistern. "There!" he said. "That'll do to put it in. It won't get out o' that, I bet you!"

"Well, I'd like to know what you want to keep it for," Sam said peevishly, and, with the suggestion of a sneer, he added, "I s'pose you think somebody'll pay about a hunderd dollars reward, or give us a medal or something, on account of a cat!"

"I don't, either!" Penrod protested hotly. "I know what I'm doin', I tell you."

"Well, what on earth——"

"I'll tell you some day, won't I?" Penrod cried. "I got my reasons for wantin' to keep this cat, and I'm goin' to keep it. *You* don't haf to ke——"

"Well, all right," said Sam shortly. "Anyways, it'll be dead if you don't hurry."

"It won't, either," Penrod returned, kneeling and peering down upon the dark water. "Listen to him! He's growlin' and spittin' away like anything! It takes a mighty fine-blooded cat to be as fierce as that. I bet you most cats would 'a' given up and drowned long ago. The water's awful cold, and I expect he was perty supprised when he lit in it."

"Herman's makin' a fuss again," said Sam. "We better get the ole cat out o' there if we're goin' to."

"Well, this is the way we'll do," Penrod said authoritatively: "I'll let you hold the trousers, Sam. You lay down and keep hold of one leg, and let the other one hang down till its end is in the water. Then you kind of swish it around till it's somewheres where the cat can get hold of it, and soon as he does, you pull it up, and be mighty careful so's it don't fall off. Then I'll grab it and stick it in the box and slam the lid down."

Rather pleased to be assigned to the trousers, Sam accordingly extended himself at full length upon the slab and proceeded to carry out Penrod's instructions. Meanwhile, Penrod, peering from above, inquired anxiously for information concerning this work of rescue.

"Can you see it, Sam? Why don't it grab hold? What's it doin' now, Sam?"

"It's spittin' at Herman's trousers," said Sam. "My gracious, but it's a fierce cat! If it's mad all the time like this, you better not ever try to pet it much. Now it's kind o' sniffin' at the trousers. It acks to me as if it was goin' to ketch holds. Yes, it's stuck one claw in 'em—— *Ow!*"

Sam uttered a blood-curdling shriek and jerked convulsively. The next instant, streaming and inconceivably gaunt, the ravening Gipsy appeared with a final bound upon Sam's shoulder. It was not in Gipsy's character to be drawn up peaceably; he had ascended the trousers and Sam's arm without assistance and in his own way. Simultaneously—for this was a notable case of everything happening at once—there was a muffled, soggy splash, and the unfortunate Herman, smit with prophecy in his seclusion, uttered a dismal yell. Penrod laid hands upon Gipsy, and, after a struggle suggestive of sailors landing a man-eating shark, succeeded in getting him into the box, and sat upon the lid thereof.

Sam had leaped to his feet, empty handed and vociferous.

"Ow, ow, *ouch!*" he shouted, as he rubbed his

suffering arm and shoulder. Then, exasperated by Herman's lamentations, he called angrily: "Oh, what *I* care for your ole britches? I guess if you'd 'a' had a cat climb up *you*, you'd 'a' dropped 'em a hunderd times over!"

However, upon excruciating entreaty, he consented to explore the surface of the water with a clothes-prop, but reported that the luckless trousers had disappeared in the depths, Herman having forgotten to remove some "fishin' sinkers" from his pockets before making the fated loan.

Penrod was soothing a lacerated wrist in his mouth.

"That's a mighty fine-blooded cat," he remarked. "I expect it'd got away from pretty near anybody, 'specially if they didn't know much about cats. Listen at him, in the box, Sam. I bet you never heard a cat growl as loud as that in your life. I shouldn't wonder it was part panther or sumpthing."

Sam began to feel more interest and less resentment.

"I tell you what we can do, Penrod," he said: "Let's take it in the stable and make the box into a cage. We can take off the hinges, and slide back the lid a little at a time, and nail some o' those laths over the front for bars."

"That's just exackly what I was goin' to say!" Penrod exclaimed. "I already thought o' that, Sam. Yessir, we'll make it just like a reg'lar circus-cage, and our good ole cat can look out from between the bars and growl. It'll come in pretty handy if we ever decide to have another show. Anyways, we'll have her in there, good and tight, where we can watch she don't get away. I got a mighty good reason to keep this cat, Sam. You'll see."

"Well, why don't you——" Sam was interrupted by a vehement appeal from the stable. "Oh, we're comin'!" he shouted. "We got to bring our cat in its cage, haven't we?"

"Listen, Herman," Penrod called absent-mindedly. "Bring us some bricks, or something awful heavy to put on the lid of our cage, so we can carry it without our good ole cat pushin' the lid open."

Herman explained with vehemence that it would not be right for him to leave the stable upon any errand until just restorations had been made. He spoke inimically of the cat, which had been the occasion of his loss, and he earnestly requested that operations with the clothes-prop be resumed in the cistern. Sam and Penrod declined, on the ground that this was absolutely proven to be of no avail, and Sam went to look for bricks.

These two boys were not unfeeling. They sympathized with Herman, but they regarded the trousers as a loss about which there was no use in making so much outcry. To them, it was part of an episode which ought to be closed. They had done their best, and Sam had not intended to drop the trousers; that was something which no one could have helped, and therefore no one was to be blamed. What they were now interested in was the construction of a circus-cage for their good ole cat.

"It's goin' to be a cage just exactly like circus-cages, Herman," Penrod said, as he and Sam set the box down on the stable floor. "You can help us nail the bars and——"

"I ain' studyin' 'bout no bars!" Herman interrupted fiercely. "What good you reckon nailin' bars go' do me if mammy holler fer me? You white boys sutn'y show me bad day! I try treat people nice, 'n'en they go th'ow my britches down cistern!"

"I did not!" Sam protested. "That ole cat just kicked 'em out o' my hand with its hind feet while its front ones were stickin' in my arm.   I bet *you'd* of——"

"Blame it on cat!" Herman sneered.   "'At's nice! Jes' looky here minute: Who'd I len' 'em britches to?   D' I len' 'em britches to thishere cat?   No, suh; you know I didn'!   You know well's any man I len' 'em britches to you—an' you tuck an' th'owed 'em down cistern!"

"Oh, *please* hush up about your old britches!" Penrod said plaintively.   "I got to think how we're goin' to fix our cage up right, and you make so much noise I can't get my mind on it.   Anyways, didn't I give you that little saw?"

"Li'l saw!" cried Herman, unmollified.   "Yes; an' thishere li'l saw go' do me lot o' good when I got to go home!"

"Why, it's only across the alley to your house, Herman!" said Sam.   "That ain't anything at all to step over there, and you've got your little saw."

"Aw right!   You jes' take off you' clo'es an' step 'cross the alley," said Herman bitterly.   "I give you li'l saw to carry!"

Penrod had begun to work upon the cage.

"Now listen here, Herman," he said: "If you'll quit talkin' so much, and kind of get settled down or sumpthing, and help us fix a good cage for our panther, well, when mamma comes home about five o'clock, I'll go and tell her there's a poor boy got his britches burned up in a fire, and how he's waitin' out in the stable for some, and I'll tell her I promised him. Well, she'll give me a pair I wore for summer; honest she will, and you can put 'em on as quick as anything."

"There, Herman," said Sam; "now you're all right again!"

"*Who* all right?" Herman complained. "I like feel sump'm' roun' my laigs befo' no five o'clock!"

"Well, you're sure to get 'em by then," Penrod promised. "It ain't winter yet, Herman. Come on and help saw these laths for the bars, Herman, and Sam and I'll nail 'em on It ain't long till five o'clock, Herman, and then you'll just feel fine!"

Herman was not convinced, but he found himself at a disadvantage in the argument. The question at issue seemed a vital one to him—and yet his two opponents evidently considered it of minor importance. Obviously, they felt that the promise for five o'clock had settled the whole matter conclusively, but to Herman this did not appear to be the fact. However, he helplessly suffered himself to be cajoled back into carpentry, though he was extremely ill at ease and talked a great deal of his misfortune. He shivered and grumbled, and, by his passionate urgings, compelled Penrod to go into the house so many times to see what time it was by the kitchen clock that both his companions almost lost patience with him.

"There!" said Penrod, returning from performing this errand for the fourth time. "It's twenty minutes after three, and I'm not goin' in to look at that ole clock again if I haf to die for it! I never heard anybody make such a fuss in my life, and I'm gettin' tired of it. Must think we want to be all night fixin' this cage for our panther! If you ask me to go and see what time it is again, Herman, I'm a-goin' to take back about askin' mamma at five o'clock, and *then* where'll you be?"

"Well, it seem like mighty long aft'noon to me," Herman sighed. "I jes' like to know what time it *is* gettin' to be now!"

"Look out!' Penrod warned him. "You heard what I was just tellin' you about how I'd take back——"

"Nemmine," Herman said hurriedly. "I wasn' astin' you. I jes' sayin' sump'm' kind o' to myse'f like."

CHAPTER XIV

CAMERA WORK IN THE JUNGLE

THE completed cage, with Gipsy behind the bars, framed a spectacle sufficiently thrilling and panther-like. Gipsy raved, "spat," struck virulently at taunting fingers, turned on his wailing siren for minutes at a time, and he gave his imitation of a dromedary almost continuously. These phenomena could be intensified in picturesqueness, the boys discovered, by rocking the cage a little, tapping it with a hammer, or raking the bars with a stick. Altogether, Gipsy was having a lively afternoon.

There came a vigorous rapping on the alley door of the stable, and Verman was admitted.

"Yay, Verman!" cried Sam Williams. "Come and look at our good ole panther!"

Another curiosity, however, claimed Verman's attention. His eyes opened wide, and he pointed at Herman's legs.

"Wha' ma' oo? Mammy hay oo hip ap hoe-woob."

188

"Mammy tell *me* git 'at stove-wood?" Herman interpreted resentfully. "How'm I go' git 'at stove-wood when my britches down bottom 'at cistern, I like you answer *me* please? You shet 'at do' behime you!"

Verman complied, and again pointing to his brother's legs, requested to be enlightened.

"Ain' I tole you once they down bottom 'at cistern?" Herman shouted, much exasperated. "You wan' know how come so, you ast Sam Williams. He say thishere cat tuck an' th'owed 'em down there!"

Sam, who was busy rocking the cage, remained cheerfully absorbed in that occupation.

"Come look at our good ole panther, Verman," he called. "I'll get this circus-cage rockin' right good, an' then——"

"Wait a minute," said Penrod; "I got sumpthing I got to think about. Quit rockin' it! I guess I got a right to think about sumpthing without havin' to go deaf, haven't I?"

Having obtained the quiet so plaintively requested, he knit his brow and gazed intently upon Verman, then upon Herman, then upon Gipsy. Evidently his idea was fermenting. He broke the silence with a shout.

"*I* know, Sam! I know what we'll do *now!*
I just thought of it, and it's goin' to be sumpthing
I bet there aren't any other boys in this town could
do, because where would they get any good ole
panther like we got, and Herman and Verman?
And they'd haf to have a dog, too—and we got our
good ole Dukie, I guess. I bet we have the greatest
ole time this afternoon we ever had in our lives!"

His enthusiasm roused the warm interest of Sam
and Verman, though Herman, remaining cold and
suspicious, asked for details.

"An' I like to hear if it's sump'm'," he concluded,
"what's go' git me my britches back outen 'at cistern!"

"Well, it ain't exackly that," said Penrod. "It's
different from that. What I'm thinkin' about,
well, for us to have it the way it ought to be, so's
you and Verman would look like natives—well,
Verman ought to take off his britches, too."

"Mo!" said Verman, shaking his head violently.
"Mo!"

"Well, wait a minute, can't you?" Sam Williams
said. "Give Penrod a chance to say what he wants
to, first, can't you? Go on, Penrod."

"Well, you know, Sam," said Penrod, turning to

"'How'm I go' git 'at stove-wood when my briches down bottom 'at cistern, I like you answer me, please.'"

this sympathetic auditor; "you remember that
movin'-pitcher show we went to, 'Fortygraphing
Wild Animals in the Jungle.' Well, Herman would-
n't have to do a thing more to look like those natives
we saw that the man called the 'beaters.' They
were dressed just about like the way he is now, and
if Verman——"

"*Mo!*" said Verman.

"Oh, *wait* a minute, Verman!" Sam entreated.
"Go on, Penrod."

"Well, we can make a mighty good jungle up in
the loft," Penrod continued eagerly. "We can
take that ole dead tree that's out in the alley and
some branches, and I bet we could have the best
jungle you ever saw. And then we'd fix up a kind
of place in there for our panther, only, of course,
we'd haf to keep him in the cage so's he wouldn't
run away, but we'd pretend he was loose. And then
you remember how they did with that calf? Well,
we'd have Duke for the tied-up calf for the panther
to come out and jump on, so they could fortygraph
him. Herman can be the chief beater, and we'll
let Verman be the other beaters, and I'll——"

"Yay!" shouted Sam Williams. "I'll be the
fortygraph man!'

"No," said Penrod; "you be the one with the gun that guards the fortygraph man, because I'm the fortygraph man already. You can fix up a mighty good gun with this carpenter shop, Sam. We'll make spears for our good ole beaters, too, and I'm goin' to make me a camera out o' that little starch-box and a bakin'-powder can that's goin' to be a mighty good ole camera. We can do lots more things——"

"Yay!" Sam cried. "Let's get started!" He paused. "Wait a minute, Penrod. Verman says he won't——"

"Well, he's got to!" said Penrod.

"I momp!" Verman insisted, almost distinctly.

They began to argue with him, but, for a time, Verman remained firm. They upheld the value of dramatic consistency, declaring that a beater dressed as completely as he was "wouldn't look like any-thing at. all." He would "spoil the whole biznuss," they said, and they praised Herman for the faithful accuracy of his costume. They also insisted that the garment in question was much too large for Verman, anyway, having been so recently worn by Herman and turned over to Verman with in-sufficient alteration, and they expressed surprise that "anybody with any sense" should make such a point of clinging to a misfit.

Herman sided against his brother in this controversy, perhaps because a certain loneliness, of which he was conscious, might be assuaged by the company of another trouserless person—or it may be that his motive was more sombre. Possibly he remembered that Verman's trousers were his own former property and might fit him in case the promise for five o'clock turned out badly. At all events, Verman finally yielded under great pressure, and consented to appear in the proper costume of the multitude of beaters it now became his duty to personify.

Shouting, the boys dispersed to begin the preparation of their jungle scene. Sam and Penrod went for branches and the dead tree, while Herman and Verman carried the panther in his cage to the loft, where the first thing that Verman did was to hang his trousers on a nail in a conspicuous and accessible spot near the doorway. And with the arrival of Penrod and Sam, panting and dragging no inconsiderable thicket after them, the coloured brethren began to take a livelier interest in things. Indeed, when Penrod, a little later, placed in their hands two spears, pointed with tin, their good spirits were entirely restored, and they even began to take a pride in being properly uncostumed beaters.

Sam's gun and Penrod's camera were entirely satisfactory, especially the latter. The camera was so attractive, in fact, that the hunter and the chief beater and all the other beaters immediately resigned and insisted upon being photographers. Each had to be given a "turn" before the jungle project could be resumed.

"Now, for goodnesses' sakes," said Penrod, taking the camera from Verman, "I hope you're done, so's we can get started doin' something like we ought to! We got to have Duke for a tied-up calf. We'll have to bring him and tie him out here in front the jungle, and then the panther'll come out and jump on him. Wait, and I'll go bring him."

Departing upon this errand, Penrod found Duke enjoying the declining rays of the sun in the front yard.

"Hyuh, Duke!" called his master, in an indulgent tone. "Come on, good ole Dukie! Come along!"

Duke rose conscientiously and followed him.

"I got him, men!" Penrod called from the stairway. "I got our good ole calf all ready to be tied up. Here he is!" And he appeared in the doorway with the unsuspecting little dog beside him.

Gipsy, who had been silent for some moments, instantly raised his banshee battlecry, and Duke yelped in horror. Penrod made a wild effort to hold him, but Duke was not to be detained. Unnatural strength and activity came to him in his delirium, and, for the second or two that the struggle lasted, his movements were too rapid for the eyes of the spectators to follow—merely a whirl and blur in the air could be seen. Then followed a sound of violent scrambling—and Penrod sprawled alone at the top of the stairs.

"Well, why'n't you come and help me?" he demanded indignantly. "I couldn't get him back now if I was to try a million years!"

"What we goin' to do about it?" Sam asked.

Penrod rose and dusted his knees. "We got to get along without any tied-up calf—that's certain! But I got to take those fortygraphs *some* way or other!"

"Me an' Verman aw ready begin 'at beatin'," Herman suggested. "You tole us we the beaters."

"Well, wait a minute," said Penrod, whose feeling for realism in drama was always alert. "I want to get a mighty good pitcher o' that ole panther this time." As he spoke, he threw open the wide door intended for the delivery of hay into the loft from the alley below. "Now, bring the cage over here by this door so's I can get a better light; it's gettin' kind of dark over where the jungle is. We'll pretend there isn't any cage there, and soon as I get him fortygraphed, I'll holler, 'Shoot, men!' Then you must shoot, Sam—and Herman, you and Verman must hammer on the cage with your spears, and holler: 'Hoo! Hoo!' and pretend you're spearin' him."

"Well, we aw ready!" said Herman. "Hoo! Hoo!"

"Wait a minute," Penrod interposed, frowningly surveying the cage. "I got to squat too much to get my camera fixed right." He assumed various solemn poses, to be interpreted as those of a photographer studying his subject. "No," he said finally; "it won't take good that way."

"My goo'ness!" Herman exclaimed. "When we goin' begin 'at beatin'?"

"Here!" Apparently Penrod had solved a weighty problem. "Bring that busted ole kitchen chair, and set the panther up on it. There! *That's* the ticket! This way, it'll make a mighty good pitcher!"

He turned to Sam importantly. "Well, Jim, is the chief and all his beaters here?"

"Yes, Bill; all here," Sam responded, with an air of loyalty.

"Well, then, I guess we're ready," said Penrod, in his deepest voice. "Beat, men."

Herman and Verman were anxious to beat. They set up the loudest uproar of which they were capable. "Hoo! Hoo! Hoo!" they bellowed, flailing the branches with their spears and stamping heavily upon the floor. Sam, carried away by the *élan* of the performance, was unable to resist joining them. "Hoo! Hoo! Hoo!" he shouted. "Hoo! Hoo! Hoo!" And as the dust rose from the floor to their stamping, the three of them produced such a din and hoo-hooing as could be made by nothing on earth except boys.

"Back, men!" Penrod called, raising his voice to the utmost. "Back for your lives. The *pa-a-anther!* Now I'm takin' his pitcher. Click, click! Shoot, men; shoot!"

"Bing! Bing!" shouted Sam, levelling his gun at the cage, while Herman and Verman hammered upon it, and Gipsy cursed boys, the world, and the day he was born. "Bing! Bing! Bing!"

"You missed him!" screamed Penrod. "Give *me* that gun!" And snatching it from Sam's unwilling hand, he levelled it at the cage.

"BING!" he roared.

Simultaneously there was the sound of another report, but this was an actual one and may best be symbolized by the statement that it was a whack. The recipient was Herman, and, outrageously surprised and pained, he turned to find himself face to face with a heavily built coloured woman who had recently ascended the stairs and approached the preoccupied hunters from the rear. In her hand was a lath, and, even as Herman turned, it was again wielded, this time upon Verman.

"*Mammy !*"

"Yes; you bettuh holler, 'Mammy!'" she panted. "My goo'ness, if yo' pappy don' lam you to-night! Ain' you got no mo' sense 'an to let white boys 'suade you play you Affikin heathums? Whah you britches?"

"Yonnuh Verman's," quavered Herman.

"Whah y'own?"

Choking, Herman answered bravely:

"'At ole cat tuck an' th'owed 'em down cistern!"

Exasperated almost beyond endurance, she lifted

" 'Bing! Bing!' shouted Sam, levelling his gun at the cage, while Herman
and Verman hammered upon it, and Gipsy cursed boys, the world, and
the day he was born"

the lath again. But unfortunately, in order to obtain a better field of action, she moved backward a little, coming in contact with the bars of the cage, a circumstance which she overlooked. More unfortunately still, the longing of the captive to express his feelings was such that he would have welcomed the opportunity to attack an elephant. He had been striking and scratching at inanimate things and at boys out of reach for the past hour, but here at last was his opportunity. He made the most of it.

"I learn you tell me cat th'owed—*ooooh!*"

The coloured woman leaped into the air like an athlete, and, turning with a swiftness astounding in one of her weight, beheld the semaphoric arm of Gipsy again extended between the bars and hopefully reaching for her. Beside herself, she lifted her right foot briskly from the ground, and allowed the sole of her shoe to come in contact with Gipsy's cage.

The cage moved from the tottering chair beneath it. It passed through the yawning hay-door and fell resoundingly to the alley below, where—as Penrod and Sam, with cries of dismay, rushed to the door and looked down—it burst asunder and dis-

gorged a large, bruised, and chastened cat. Gipsy
paused and bent one strange look upon the broken
box. Then he shook his head and departed up the
alley, the two boys watching him till he was out of
sight.

Before they turned, a harrowing procession issued
from the carriage-house doors beneath them. Herman came first, hurriedly completing a temporary
security, in Verman's trousers. Verman followed,
after a little reluctance, which departed coincidentally with some inspiriting words from the rear. He
crossed the alley hastily, and his mammy stalked
behind, using constant eloquence and a frequent lath.
They went into the small house across the way and
closed the door.

Then Sam turned to Penrod.

"Penrod," he said thoughtfully, "was it on account of fortygraphing in the jungle you wanted to
keep that cat?"

"No; that was a mighty fine-blooded cat. We'd
of made some money."

Sam jeered.

"You mean when we'd sell tickets to look at it
in its cage?"

Penrod shook his head, and if Gipsy could have

overheard and understood his reply, that atrabilious spirit, almost broken by the events of the day, might have considered this last blow the most overwhelming of all.

"No," said Penrod; "when she had kittens."

CHAPTER XV

O N MONDAY morning Penrod's faith in the coming of another Saturday was flaccid and lustreless. Those Japanese lovers who were promised a reunion after ten thousand years in separate hells were brighter with hope than he was. On Monday Penrod was virtually an agnostic.

Nowhere upon his shining morning face could have been read any eager anticipation of useful knowledge. Of course he had been told that school was for his own good; in fact, he had been told and told and told, but the words conveying this information, meaningless at first, assumed, with each repetition, more and more the character of dull and unsolicited insult.

He was wholly unable to imagine circumstances, present or future, under which any of the instruction and training he was now receiving could be of the slightest possible use or benefit to himself; and when he was informed that such circumstances would frequently arise in his later life, he but felt the slur upon his coming manhood and its power to prevent any such unpleasantness.

If it were possible to place a romantic young Broadway actor and athlete under hushing supervision for six hours a day, compelling him to bend his unremittent attention upon the city directory of Sheboygan, Wisconsin, he could scarce be expected to respond genially to frequent statements that the compulsion was all for his own good. On the contrary, it might be reasonable to conceive his response as taking the form of action, which is precisely the form that Penrod's smouldering impulse yearned to take.

To Penrod school was merely a state of confinement, envenomed by mathematics. For interminable periods he was forced to listen to information concerning matters about which he had no curiosity whatever; and he had to read over and over the dullest passages in books that bored him into stupors, while always there overhung the preposterous task of improvising plausible evasions to conceal the fact that he did not know what he had no wish to know. Likewise, he must always be prepared to avoid incriminating replies to questions which he

felt nobody had a real and natural right to ask him.
And when his gorge rose and his inwards revolted,
the hours became a series of ignoble misadventures
and petty disgraces strikingly lacking in privacy.

It was usually upon Wednesday that his sufferings
culminated; the nervous strength accumulated during the holiday hours at the end of the week would
carry him through Monday and Tuesday, but by
Wednesday it seemed ultimately proven that the
next Saturday actually *never* was coming, "this
time," and the strained spirit gave way. Wednesday
was the day averaging highest in Penrod's list of
absences, but the time came when he felt that the
advantages attendant upon his Wednesday "sick
headache" did not compensate for its inconven-
iences.

For one thing, this illness had become so sym-
metrically recurrent that even the cook felt that he
was pushing it too far, and the liveliness of her expression, when he was able to leave his couch and take
the air in the backyard at about ten o'clock, became
more disagreeable to him with each convalescence.
There visibly increased, too, about the whole household, an atmosphere of uncongeniality and suspicion
so pronounced that every successive illness was neces-

sarily more severe, and at last the patient felt obliged to remain bedded until almost eleven, from time to time giving forth pathetic little sounds eloquent of anguish triumphing over Stoic endurance, yet lacking a certain conviction of utterance.

Finally, his father enacted, and his mother applied, a new and distinctly special bit of legislation, explaining it with simple candor to the prospective beneficiary.

"Whenever you really *are* sick," they said, "you can go out and play as soon as you're well—that is, if it happens on Saturday. But when you're sick on a school-day, you'll stay in bed till the next morning. This is going to do you good, Penrod."

Physically, their opinion appeared to be affirmed, for Wednesday after Wednesday passed without any recurrence of the attack, but the spiritual strain may have been damaging. And it should be added that if Penrod's higher nature did suffer from the strain, he was not unique. For, confirming the effect of Wednesday upon boys.in general, it is probable that, if full statistics concerning cats were available, they would show that cats dread Wednesdays, and that their fear is shared by other animals, and would be shared, to an extent by windows, if windows possessed nervous systems. Nor must this probable apprehension on the part of cats and the like be thought mere superstition. Cats have superstitions, it is true, but certain actions inspired by the sight of a boy with a missile in his hand are better evidence of the workings of logic upon a practical nature than of faith in the supernatural.

Moreover, the attention of family physicians and specialists should be drawn to these significant though obscure phenomena; for the suffering of cats is a barometer of the nerve-pressure of boys, and it may be accepted as sufficiently established that Wednesday—after school-hours—is the worst time for cats.

After the promulgation of that parental edict, "You'll stay in bed till the next morning," four weeks went by unflawed by a single absence from the field of duty, but, when the fifth Wednesday came, Penrod held sore debate within himself before he finally rose. In fact, after rising, and while actually engaged with his toilet, he tentatively emitted the series of the little moans that was his wonted preliminary to a quiet holiday at home; and the sound was heard (as intended) by Mr. Schofield, who was passing Penrod's door on his way to breakfast.

"*All* right!" said the father, making use of peculiar

and unnecessary emphasis. "Stay in bed till to-morrow morning. Castor-oil, this time, too."

Penrod had not hoped much for his experiment; nevertheless, his rebellious blood was sensibly inflamed by the failure, and he accompanied his dressing with a low murmuring—apparently a bitter dialogue between himself and some unknown but powerful patron.

Thus he muttered:

"Well, they better *not!*" "Well, what can I *do* about it?" "Well, *I'd* show 'em!" "Well, I *will* show 'em!" "Well, you *ought* to show 'em; that's the way *I* do! I just shake 'em around, and say, 'Here! I guess you don't know who you're talkin' to, that way! You better look out!'" "Well, that's the way *I'm* goin' to do!" "Well, go on and *do* it, then!" "Well, I *am* goin'——"

The door of the next room was slightly ajar; now it swung wide, and Margaret appeared.

"Penrod, what on earth are you talking about?"

"Nothin'. None o' your——"

"Well, hurry to breakfast, then; it's getting late."

Lightly she went, humming a tune, leaving the door of her room open; and the eyes of Penrod, as he donned his jacket, chanced to fall upon her desk, where she had thoughtlessly left a letter—a private missive just begun, and intended solely for the eyes of Mr. Robert Williams, a senior at a far university.

In such a fashion is coincidence the architect of misfortune. Penrod's class in English composition had been instructed, the previous day, to concoct at home and bring to class on Wednesday morning, "a model letter to a friend on some subject of general interest." Penalty for omission to perform this simple task was definite; whosoever brought no letter would inevitably be "kept in" after school, that afternoon, until the letter was written, and it was precisely a premonition of this misfortune which had prompted Penrod to attempt his experimental moaning upon his father, for, alas! he had equipped himself with no model letter, nor any letter whatever.

In stress of this kind, a boy's creed is that anything is worth a try; but his eye for details is poor. He sees the future too sweepingly and too much as he would have it, seldom providing against inconsistencies of evidence which may damage him. For instance, there is a well-known case of two brothers who exhibited to their parents, with pathetic confidence, several imported dried herring on a string, as a proof that the afternoon had been spent, not at a forbidden circus, but with hook and line upon the banks of a neighbouring brook. ·

So with Penrod. He had vital need of a letter, and there, before his eyes, upon Margaret's desk, was apparently the precise thing he needed!

From below rose the voice of his mother urging him to the breakfast-table, warning him that he stood in danger of tardiness at school; he was pressed for time, and acted upon an inspiration which failed to prompt him even to read the letter.

Hurriedly he wrote "Dear freind" at the top of the page Margaret had partially filled. Then he signed himself, "Yours respectfuly, Penrod Schofield" at the bottom, and enclosed the missive within a battered volume entitled, "Principles of English Composition." With that and other books compacted by a strap, he descended to a breakfast somewhat oppressive but undarkened by any misgivings concerning a "letter to a friend on some subject of general interest." He felt that a difficulty had been encountered and satisfactorily disposed of; the matter could now be dismissed from his mind. He had plenty of other difficulties to take its place.

No; he had no misgivings, nor was he assailed by anything unpleasant in that line, even when the hour struck for the class in English composition. If he had been two or three years older, experience might have warned him to take at least the precaution of copying his offering, so that it would appear in his own handwriting when he "handed it in," but Penrod had not even glanced at it.

"I think," said Miss Spence, "I will ask several of you to read your letters aloud before you hand them in. Clara Raypole, you may read yours."

Penrod was bored but otherwise comfortable; he had no apprehension that he might be included in the "several," especially as Miss Spence's beginning with Clara Raypole, a star performer, indicated that her selection of readers would be made from the conscientious and proficient division at the head of the class. He listened stoically to the beginning of the first letter, though he was conscious of a dull resentment, inspired mainly by the perfect complacency of Miss Raypole's voice.

"'Dear Cousin Sadie,'" she began smoothly, "'I thought I would write you to-day on some subject of general interest, and so I thought I would tell you about the subject of our court-house. It is a very fine building situated in the centre of the city, and a visit to the building after school hours well

repays for the visit. Upon entrance we find upon
our left the office of the county clerk and upon our
right a number of windows affording a view of the
street. And so we proceed, finding on both sides
much of general interest. The building was begun in
1886 A. D. and it was through in 1887 A. D. It is four
stories high and made of stone, pressed brick, wood,
and tiles, with a tower, or cupola, one hundred
and twenty-seven feet seven inches from the ground.
Among other subjects of general interest told by
the janitor, we learn that the architect of the
building was a man named Flanner, and the foun-
dations extend fifteen feet five inches under the
ground——'"

Penrod was unable to fix his attention upon these
statistics; he began moodily to twist a button of his
jacket and to concentrate a new-born and obscure
but lasting hatred upon the court-house. Miss
Raypole's glib voice continued to press upon his
ears, but, by keeping his eyes fixed upon the twisting
button he had accomplished a kind of self-hypnosis,
or mental anæsthesia, and was but dimly aware of
what went on about him.

The court-house was finally exhausted by its
visitor, who resumed her seat and submitted with

beamish grace to praise. Then Miss Spence said, in a favourable manner:

"Georgie Bassett, you may read your letter next."

The neat Georgie rose, nothing loath, and began: "'Dear Teacher——'"

There was a slight titter, which Miss Spence suppressed. Georgie was not at all discomfited.

"'My mother says,'" he continued, reading his manuscript, "'we should treat our teacher as a friend, and so *I* will write *you* a letter.'"

This penetrated Penrod's trance, and he lifted his eyes to fix them upon the back of Georgie Bassett's head in a long and inscrutable stare. It was inscrutable, and yet if Georgie had been sensitive to thought waves, it is probable that he would have uttered a loud shriek, but he remained placidly unaware, continuing:

"'I thought I would write you about a subject of general interest, and so I will write you about the flowers. There are many kinds of flowers, spring flowers, and summer flowers, and autumn flowers, but no winter flowers. Wild flowers grow in the woods, and it is nice to hunt them in springtime, and we must remember to give some to the poor and hospitals, also. Flowers can be made to grow in flower-beds and placed in vases in houses. There are many names for flowers, but *I* call them "nature's ornaments"——'"

Penrod's gaze had relaxed, drooped to his button again, and his lethargy was renewed. The outer world grew vaguer; voices seemed to drone at a distance; sluggish time passed heavily—but some of it did pass.

"Penrod!"

Miss Spence's searching eye had taken note of the bent head and the twisting button. She found it necessary to speak again.

"Penrod Schofield!"

He came languidly to life.

"Ma'am?"

"You may read your letter."

"Yes'm."

And he began to paw clumsily among his books, whereupon Miss Spence's glance fired with suspicion.

"Have you prepared one?" she demanded.

"Yes'm," said Penrod dreamily.

"But you're going to find you forgot to bring it, aren't you?"

"I got it," said Penrod, discovering the paper in his "Principles of English Composition."

"Well, we'll listen to what you've found time to prepare," she said, adding coldly, "for once!"

The frankest pessimism concerning Penrod permeated the whole room; even the eyes of those whose letters had not met with favour turned upon him with obvious assurance that here was every prospect of a performance which would, by comparison, lend a measure of credit to the worst preceding it. But Penrod was unaffected by the general gaze; he rose, still blinking from his lethargy, and in no true sense wholly alive.

He had one idea: to read as rapidly as possible, so as to be done with the task, and he began in a high-pitched monotone, reading with a blind mind and no sense of the significance of the words.

"'Dear friend,'" he declaimed. "'You call me beautiful, but I am not really beautiful, and there are times when I doubt if I am even pretty, though perhaps my hair is beautiful, and if it is true that my eyes are like blue stars in heaven——'"

Simultaneously he lost his breath and there burst upon him a perception of the results to which he

"'Dear friend,' he declaimed, 'you call me beautiful, but I am not really beautiful'."

was being committed by this calamitous reading. And also simultaneous was the outbreak of the class into cachinnations of delight, severely repressed by the perplexed but indignant Miss Spence.

"Go on!" she commanded grimly, when she had restored order.

"Ma'am?" he gulped, looking wretchedly upon the rosy faces all about him.

"Go on with the description of yourself," she said. "We'd like to hear some more about your eyes being like blue stars in heaven."

Here many of Penrod's little comrades were forced to clasp their faces tightly in both hands; and his dismayed gaze, in refuge, sought the treacherous paper in his hand.

What it beheld there was horrible.

"Proceed!" said Miss Spence.

"'I—often think,'" he faltered, "'and a-a tree-more thu-thrills my bein' when I *recall* your last words to me that last—that last—that——'"

"*Go on!*"

"'That last evening in the moonlight when you —you—you——'"

"Penrod," Miss Spence said dangerously, "you go on, and stop that stammering."

"'You—you said you would wait for—for years to—to—to—to——' "

"*Penrod !*"

"'To win me!'" the miserable Penrod managed to gasp. "'I should not have pre—premitted—permitted you to speak so until we have our—our parents' con-consent; but oh, how sweet it——'" He exhaled a sigh of agony, and then concluded briskly, "'Yours respectfully, Penrod Schofield.'"

But Miss Spence had at last divined something, for she knew the Schofield family.

"Bring me that letter!" she said.

And the scarlet boy passed forward between rows of mystified but immoderately uplifted children.

Miss Spence herself grew rather pink as she examined the missive, and the intensity with which she afterward extended her examination to cover the complete field of Penrod Schofield caused him to find a remote centre of interest whereon to rest his embarrassed gaze. She let him stand before her throughout a silence, equalled, perhaps, by the tenser pauses during trials for murder, and then, containing herself, she sweepingly gestured him to the pillory—a chair upon the platform, facing the school.

Here he suffered for the unusual term of an hour, with many jocular and cunning eyes constantly upon him; and, when he was released at noon, horrid shouts and shrieks pursued him every step of his homeward way. For his laughter-loving little schoolmates spared him not—neither boy nor girl.

"Yay, Penrod!" they shouted. "How's your beautiful hair?" And, "Hi, Penrod! When you goin' to get your parents' consent?" And, "Say, blue stars in heaven, how's your beautiful eyes?" And, "Say, Penrod, how's your tree-mores?" "Does your tree-mores thrill your bein', Penrod?" And many other facetious inquiries, hard to bear in public.

And when he reached the temporary shelter of his home, he experienced no relief upon finding that Margaret was out for lunch. He was as deeply embittered toward her as toward any other, and, considering her largely responsible for his misfortune, he would have welcomed an opportunity to show her what he thought of her.

CHAPTER XVI

WEDNESDAY MADNESS

HOW long he was "kept in" after school that afternoon is not a matter of record, but it was long. Before he finally appeared upon the street, he had composed an ample letter on a subject of general interest, namely "School Life," under the supervision of Miss Spence; he had also received some scorching admonitions in respect to honourable behaviour regarding other people's letters; and Margaret's had been returned to him with severe instructions to bear it straight to the original owner accompanied by full confession and apology. As a measure of insurance that these things be done, Miss Spence stated definitely her intention to hold a conversation by telephone with Margaret that evening. Altogether, the day had been unusually awful, even for Wednesday, and Penrod left the school-house with the heart of an anarchist throbbing in his hot bosom. It were more accurate, indeed, to liken him to the anarchist's characteristic weapon; for, as Penrod came out to the street he was, in all inward respects, a bomb, loaded and ticking.

He walked moodily, with a visible aspect of soreness. A murmurous sound was thick about his head, wherefore it is to be surmised that he communed with his familiar, and one vehement, oft-repeated phrase beat like a tocsin of revolt upon the air: "Daw-gone 'em!"

He meant everybody—the universe.

Particularly included, evidently, was a sparrow, offensively cheerful upon a lamp-post. This self-centred little bird allowed a pebble to pass overhead and remained unconcerned, but, a moment later, feeling a jar beneath his feet, and hearing the tinkle of falling glass, he decided to leave. Similarly, and at the same instant, Penrod made the same decision, and the sparrow in flight took note of a boy likewise in flight.

The boy disappeared into the nearest alley and emerged therefrom, breathless, in the peaceful vicinity of his own home. He entered the house, clumped upstairs and down, discovered Margaret reading a book in the library, and flung the accursed letter toward her with loathing.

"You can take the old thing," he said bitterly. "*I* don't want it!"

And before she was able to reply, he was out of the room. The next moment he was out of the house.

"Daw-*gone* 'em!" he said.

And then, across the street, his soured eye fell upon his true comrade and best friend leaning against a picket fence and holding desultory converse with Mabel Rorebeck, an attractive member of the Friday Afternoon Dancing Class, that hated organization of which Sam and Penrod were both members. Mabel was a shy little girl, but Penrod had a vague understanding that Sam considered her two brown pigtails beautiful.

Howbeit, Sam had never told his love; he was, in fact, sensitive about it. This meeting with the lady was by chance, and although it afforded exquisite moments, his heart was beating in an unaccustomed manner, and he was suffering from embarrassment, being at a loss, also, for subjects of conversation. It is, indeed, no easy matter to chat easily with a person, however lovely and beloved, who keeps her face turned the other way, maintains one foot in rapid and continuous motion through an arc seemingly perilous to her equilibrium, and confines her responses, both affirmative and negative, to "Uh-huh."

Altogether, Sam was sufficiently nervous without

any help from Penrod, and it was with pure horror
that he heard his own name and Mabel's shrieked
upon the ambient air with viperish insinuation.

"Sam-my and May-bul! *Oh*, oh!"

Sam started violently. Mabel ceased to swing her
foot, and both, encarnadined, looked up and down and
everywhere for the invisible but well-known owner of
that voice. It came again, in taunting mockery:

> "Sammy's mad, and I am glad,
> And I know what will please him:
> A bottle o' wine to make him shine,
> And Mabel Rorebeck to squeeze him!"

"Fresh ole thing!" said Miss Rorebeck, becoming
articulate. And, unreasonably including Sam in her
indignation, she tossed her head at him with an un-
mistakable effect of scorn. She began to walk away.

"Well, Mabel," said Sam plaintively, following, "it
ain't *my* fault. *I* didn't do anything. It's Penrod."

"I don't care," she began pettishly, when the
viperish voice was again lifted:

> "Oh, oh, oh!
> Who's your beau?
> Guess *I* know:
> Mabel and Sammy, oh, oh, oh!
> *I* caught you!"

Then Mabel did one of those things which eternally perplex the slower sex. She deliberately made a face, not at the tree behind which Penrod was lurking, but at the innocent and heart-wrung Sam. "You needn't come limpin' after *me*, Sam Williams!" she said, though Sam was approaching upon two perfectly sound legs. And then she ran away at the top of her speed.

"Run, nigger, run!" Penrod began inexcusably. But Sam cut the persecutions short at this point. Stung to fury, he charged upon the sheltering tree in the Schofields' yard.

Ordinarily, at such a juncture, Penrod would have fled, keeping his own temper and increasing the heat of his pursuer's by back-flung jeers. But this was Wednesday, and he was in no mood to run from Sam. He stepped away from the tree, awaiting the onset.

"Well, what you goin' to do so much?" he said.

Sam did not pause to proffer the desired information. "Tcha got'ny *sense!*" was the total extent of his vocal preliminaries before flinging himself headlong upon the taunter; and the two boys went to the ground together. Embracing, they rolled, they pommelled, they hammered, they kicked. Alas, this was a fight.

They rose, flailing awhile, then renewed their embrace, and, grunting, bestowed themselves anew upon our ever too receptive Mother Earth. Once more upon their feet, they beset each other sorely, dealing many great blows, ofttimes upon the air, but with sufficient frequency upon resentful flesh. Tears were jolted to the rims of eyes, but technically they did not weep. "Got'ny sense," was repeated chokingly many, many times; also, "Dern ole fool!" and, "I'll *show* you!"

The peacemaker who appeared upon the animated scene was Penrod's great-uncle Slocum. This elderly relative had come to call upon Mrs. Schofield, and he was well upon his way to the front door when the mutterings of war among some shrubberies near the fence caused him to deflect his course in benevolent agitation.

"Boys! Boys! Shame, boys!" he said, but, as the originality of these expressions did not prove striking enough to attract any great attention from the combatants, he felt obliged to assume a share in the proceedings. It was a share entailing greater activity than he had anticipated, and, before he managed to separate the former friends, he intercepted bodily an amount of violence to which he was wholly unaccustomed. Additionally, his attire was disarranged; his hat was no longer upon his head, and his temper was in a bad way. In fact, as his hat flew off, he made use of words which, under less extreme circumstances, would have caused both boys to feel a much profounder interest than they did in great-uncle Slocum.

"I'll *get* you!" Sam babbled. "Don't you ever dare to speak to me again, Penrod Schofield, long as you live, or I'll whip you worse'n I have this time!"

Penrod squawked. For the moment he was incapable of coherent speech, and then, failing in a convulsive attempt to reach his enemy, his fury culminated upon an innocent object which had never done him the slightest harm. Great-uncle Slocum's hat lay upon the ground close by, and Penrod was in that state of irritation which seeks an outlet too blindly—as people say, he "*had* to do *something !*" He kicked great-uncle Slocum's hat with such sweep and precision that it rose swiftly, and, breasting the autumn breeze, passed over the fence and out into the street.

Great-uncle Slocum uttered a scream of anguish, and, immediately ceasing to peacemake, ran forth to a more important rescue; but the conflict was not renewed. Sanity had returned to Sam Williams; he was awed by this colossal deed of Penrod's and filled with horror at the thought that he might be held as accessory to it. Fleetly he fled, pursued as far as the gate by the whole body of Penrod, and thereafter by Penrod's voice alone.

"You *better* run! You wait till I catch you! You'll see what you get next time! Don't you ever speak to me again as long as you——"

Here he paused abruptly, for great-uncle Slocum had recovered his hat and was returning toward the gate. After one glance at great-uncle Slocum Penrod did not linger to attempt any explanation—there are times when even a boy can see that apologies would seem out of place. This one ran round the house to the backyard.

Here he was enthusiastically greeted by Duke. "You get away from me!" said Penrod hoarsely, and with terrible gestures he repulsed the faithful animal, who retired philosophically to the stable, while his master let himself out of the back gate. Penrod had decided to absent himself from home for the time being.

The sky was gray, and there were hints of coming dusk in the air; it was an hour suited to his

turbulent soul, and he walked with a sombre swagger. "Ran like a c'ardy-calf!" he sniffed, half
aloud, alluding to the haste of Sam Williams in
departure. "All he is, ole c'ardy-calf!"

Then, as he proceeded up the alley, a hated cry
smote his ears: "Hi, Penrod! How's your tree-
mores?" And two jovial schoolboy faces appeared
above a high board fence. "How's your beautiful
hair, Penrod?" they vociferated. "When you goin'
to git your parents' consent? What makes you think
you're only pretty, ole blue stars?"

Penrod looked about feverishly for a missile, and
could find none to his hand, but the surface of the
alley sufficed; he made mud balls and fiercely bom-
barded the vociferous fence. Naturally, hostile
mud balls presently issued from behind this bar-
ricade; and thus a campaign developed which offered
a picture not unlike a cartoonist's sketch of a political
campaign, wherein this same material is used for
the decoration of opponents. But Penrod had been
unwise; he was outnumbered, and the hostile forces
held the advantageous side of the fence.

Mud balls can be hard as well as soggy; some of
those that reached Penrod were of no inconsiderable
weight and substance, and they made him grunt

despite himself. Finally, one, at close range, struck him in the pit of the stomach, whereupon he clasped himself about the middle silently, and executed some steps in seeming imitation of a quaint Indian dance.

His plight being observed through a knothole, his enemies climbed upon the fence and regarded him seriously.

"Aw, *you're* all right, ain't you, old tree-mores?" inquired one.

"I'll *show* you!" bellowed Penrod, recovering his breath; and he hurled a fat ball—thoughtfully retained in hand throughout his agony—to such effect that his interrogator disappeared backward from the fence without having taken any initiative of his own in the matter. His comrade impulsively joined him upon the ground, and the battle continued.

Through the gathering dusk it went on. It waged but the hotter as darkness made aim more difficult— and still Penrod would not be driven from the field. Panting, grunting, hoarse from returning insults, fighting on and on, an indistinguishable figure in the gloom, he held the back alley against all comers.

For such a combat darkness has one great advantage, but it has an equally important disadvantage—

the combatant cannot see to aim; on the other hand, he cannot see to dodge. And all the while Penrod was receiving two for one. He became heavy with mud. Plastered, impressionistic, and sculpturesque, there was about him a quality of the tragic, of the magnificent. He resembled a sombre masterpiece by Rodin. No one could have been quite sure what he was meant for.

Dinner bells tinkled in houses. Then they were rung from kitchen doors. Calling voices came urging from the distance, calling boys' names into the darkness. They called, and a note of irritation seemed to mar their beauty.

Then bells were rung again—and the voices renewed appeals more urgent, much more irritated. They called and called and called.

Thud ! went the mud balls.

Thud! Thud! Blunk!

"*Oof !*" said Penrod.

. . . Sam Williams, having dined with his family at their usual hour, seven, slipped unostentatiously out of the kitchen door, as soon as he could, after the conclusion of the meal, and quietly betook himself to the Schofields' corner.

Here he stationed himself where he could see all avenues of approach to the house, and waited. Twenty minutes went by, and then Sam became suddenly alert and attentive, for the arc-light revealed a small, grotesque figure slowly approaching along the sidewalk. It was brown in colour, shaggy and indefinite in form; it limped excessively, and paused to rub itself, and to meditate.

Peculiar as the thing was, Sam had no doubt as to its identity. He advanced.

"'Lo, Penrod," he said cautiously, and with a shade of formality.

Penrod leaned against the fence, and, lifting one leg, tested the knee-joint by swinging his foot back and forth, a process evidently provocative of a little pain. Then he rubbed the left side of his encrusted face, and, opening his mouth to its whole capacity as an aperture, moved his lower jaw slightly from side to side, thus triumphantly settling a question in his own mind as to whether or no a suspected dislocation had taken place.

Having satisfied himself on these points, he examined both shins delicately by the sense of touch, and carefully tested the capacities of his neck-muscles to move his head in a wonted manner.

Then he responded somewhat gruffly:

"'Lo!"

"Where you been?" Sam said eagerly, his formality vanishing.

"Havin' a mud-fight."

"I guess you did!" Sam exclaimed, in a low voice. "What you goin' to tell your——"

"Oh, nothin'."

"Your sister telephoned to our house to see if I knew where you were," said Sam. "She told me if I saw you before you got home to tell you sumpthing, but not to say anything about it. She said Miss Spence had telephoned to her, but *she* said for me to tell you it was all right about that letter, and she wasn't goin' to tell your mother and father on you, so you needn't say anything about it to 'em."

"All right," said Penrod indifferently.

"She says you're goin' to be in enough trouble without that," Sam went on. "You're goin' to catch fits about your Uncle Slocum's hat, Penrod."

"Well, I guess I know it."

"And about not comin' home to dinner, too. Your mother telephoned twice to mamma while we were eatin' to see if you'd come in our house. And when they *see* you—*my*, but you're goin' to get the *dickens*, Penrod!"

Penrod seemed unimpressed, though he was well aware that Sam's prophecy was no unreasonable one.

"Well, I guess I know it," he repeated casually. And he moved slowly toward his own gate.

His friend looked after him curiously—then, as the limping figure fumbled clumsily with bruised fingers at the latch of the gate, there sounded a little solicitude in Sam's voice.

"Say, Penrod, how—how do you feel?"

"What?"

"Do you feel pretty bad?"

"No," said Penrod, and, in spite of what awaited him beyond the lighted portals just ahead, he spoke the truth. His nerves were rested, and his soul was at peace. His Wednesday madness was over.

"No," said Penrod; "I feel bully!"

CHAPTER XVII

PENROD'S BUSY DAY

ALTHOUGH the pressure had thus been relieved and Penrod found peace with himself, nevertheless there were times during the rest of that week when he felt a strong distaste for Margaret. His schoolmates frequently reminded him of such phrases in her letter as they seemed least able to forget, and for hours after each of these experiences he was unable to comport himself with human courtesy when constrained (as at dinner) to remain for any length of time in the same room with her. But by Sunday these moods had seemed to pass; he attended church in her close company, and had no thought of the troubles brought upon him by her correspondence with a person who throughout remained unknown to him.

Penrod slumped far down in the pew with his knees against the back of that in front, and he also languished to one side, so that the people sitting behind were afforded a view of him consisting of a little hair and one bored ear. The sermon—a noble one, searching and eloquent—was but a persistent sound in that ear, though, now and then, Penrod's attention would be caught by some detached portion of a sentence, when his mind would dwell dully upon the phrases for a little while—and lapse into a torpor. At intervals his mother, without turning her head, would whisper, "Sit up, Penrod," causing him to sigh profoundly and move his shoulders about an inch, this mere gesture of compliance exhausting all the energy that remained to him.

The black backs and gray heads of the elderly men in the congregation oppressed him; they gave him a lethargic and indefinite feeling that he was immersed among lives of repellent dullness. But he should have been grateful to the lady with the artificial cherries upon her hat. His gaze lingered there, wandered away, and hopelessly returned again and again, to be a little refreshed by the glossy scarlet of the cluster of tiny globes. He was not so fortunate as to be drowsy; that would have brought him some relief—and yet, after a while, his eyes became slightly glazed; he saw dimly, and what he saw was distorted.

The church had been built in the early 'Seventies, and it contained some naïve stained glass of that period.´ ‹ The arch at the top of a window facing Penrod was filled with a gigantic Eye. Of oyster-white and raw blues and reds, inflamed by the pouring sun, it had held an awful place in the infantile life of Penrod Schofield, for in his tenderer years he accepted it without question as the literal Eye of Deity. He had been informed that the church was the divine dwelling—and there was the Eye!

Nowadays, being no longer a little child, he had somehow come to know better without being told, and though the great flaming Eye was no longer the terrifying thing it had been to him during his childhood, it nevertheless retained something of its ominous character.´ It made him feel spied upon, and its awful glare still pursued him, sometimes, as he was falling asleep at night. When he faced the window his feeling was one of dull resentment.

His own glazed eyes, becoming slightly crossed with an *ennui* which was peculiarly intense this morning, rendered the Eye more monstrous than it was. It expanded to horrible size, growing mountainous; it turned into a volcano in the tropics, and yet it stared at him, indubitably an Eye implacably hostile to all rights of privacy forever. Penrod blinked and clinched his eyelids to be rid of this dual image, and he managed to shake off the volcano. Then, lowering the angle of his glance, he saw something most remarkable—and curiously out of place.

An inverted white soup-plate was lying miraculously balanced upon the back of a pew a little distance in front of him, and upon the upturned bottom of the soup plate was a brown cocoanut. Mildly surprised, Penrod yawned, and, in the effort to straighten his eyes, came to life temporarily. The cocoanut was revealed as Georgie Bassett's head, and the soup-plate as Georgie's white collar. Georgie was sitting up straight, as he always did in church, and Penrod found this vertical rectitude unpleasant. He knew that he had more to fear from the Eye than Georgie had, and he was under the impression (a correct one) that Georgie felt on intimate terms with it and was actually fond of it.

Penrod himself would have maintained that he was fond of it, if he had been asked. He would have said so because he feared to say otherwise; and the truth is that he never consciously looked at the Eye disrespectfully. He would have been alarmed if he thought the Eye had any way of finding out how he really felt about it. When not off his guard, he always looked at it placatively.

By and by, he sagged so far to the left that he had symptoms of a "stitch in the side," and, rousing himself, sat partially straight for several moments. Then he rubbed his shoulders slowly from side to side against the back of the seat, until his mother whispered, "Don't do that, Penrod."

Upon this, he allowed himself to slump inwardly till the curve in the back of his neck rested against the curved top of the back of the seat. It was a congenial fit, and Penrod again began to move slowly from side to side, finding the friction soothing. Even so slight a pleasure was denied him by a husky, "Stop that!" from his father.

Penrod sighed, and slid farther down. He scratched his head, his left knee, his right biceps, and his left ankle, after which he scratched his right knee, his right ankle, and his left biceps. Then he said, "Oh, hum!" unconsciously, but so loudly that there was a reproving stir in the neighbourhood of the Schofield pew, and his father looked at him angrily.

Finally, his nose began to trouble him. It itched, and after scratching it, he rubbed it harshly. Another "Stop that!" from his father proved of no avail, being greeted by a desperate-sounding whisper, "I *got* to!"

And, continuing to rub his nose with his right hand, Penrod began to search his pockets with his left. The quest proving fruitless, he rubbed his nose with his left hand and searched with his right. Then he abandoned his nose and searched feverishly with both hands, going through all of his pockets several times.

"What *do* you want?" whispered his mother.

But Margaret had divined his need, and she passed him her own handkerchief. This was both thoughtful and thoughtless—the latter because Margaret was in the habit of thinking that she became faint in crowds, especially at the theatre or in church, and she had just soaked her handkerchief with spirits of ammonia from a small phial which she carried in her muff.

Penrod hastily applied the handkerchief to his nose and even more hastily exploded. He sneezed stupendously; he choked, sneezed again, wept, passed into a light convulsion of coughing and sneezing together—a mergence of sound which attracted much attention—and, after a few recurrent spasms, convalesced into a condition marked by silent tears and only sporadic instances of sneezing.

By this time his family were unanimously scarlet —his father and mother with mortification, and

Margaret with the effort to control the almost ir-
resistible mirth which the struggles and vociferations
of Penrod had inspired within her. And yet her
heart misgave her, for his bloodshot and tearful
eyes were fixed upon her from the first and remained
upon her, even when half-blinded with his agony;
and their expression—as terrible as that of the win-
dowed Eye confronting her—was not for an instant
to be misunderstood. Absolutely, he considered
that she had handed him the ammonia-soaked
handkerchief deliberately and with malice, and
well she knew that no power on earth could
now or at any time henceforth persuade him otherwise.

"Of course I didn't mean it, Penrod," she said,
at the first opportunity upon their homeward way. "I
didn't notice—that is, I didn't think——" Unfortunately for the effect of sincerity which she hoped
to produce, her voice became tremulous and her
shoulders moved suspiciously.

"Just you wait! You'll see!" he prophesied, in a
voice now choking, not with ammonia, but with
emotion. "Poison a person, and then laugh in his
face!"

He spake no more until they had reached their

own house, though she made some further futile
efforts at explanation and apology.

And after brooding abysmally throughout the
meal that followed, he disappeared from the sight
of his family, having answered with one frightful
look his mother's timid suggestion that it was almost
time for Sunday-school. He retired to his eyry—
the sawdust box in the empty stable—and there gave
rein to his embittered imaginings, incidentally form-
ing many plans for Margaret.

Most of these were much too elaborate, but one
was so alluring that he dwelt upon it, working out
the details with gloomy pleasure, even after he had
perceived its defects. It involved a considerable
postponement—in fact, until Margaret should have
become the mother of a boy about Penrod's present
age. This boy would be precisely like Georgie
Bassett—Penrod conceived that as inevitable—and,
like Georgie, he would be his mother's idol. Penrod
meant to take him to church and force him to blow
his nose with an ammonia-soaked handkerchief in
the presence of the Eye and all the congregation.

Then Penrod intended to say to this boy, after
church, "Well, that's exackly what your mother did
to me, and if you don't like it, you better look out!"

And the real Penrod in the sawdust, box clenched his fists. "Come ahead, then!" he muttered. "You talk too much!" Whereupon, the Penrod of his dream gave Margaret's puny son a contemptuous thrashing under the eyes of his mother, who besought in vain for mercy. This plan was finally dropped, not because of any lingering nepotism within Penrod, but because his injury called for action less belated.

One after another, he thought of impossible things; one after another, he thought of things merely inane and futile, for he was trying to do something beyond his power. Penrod was never brilliant, or even successful, save by inspiration.

At four o'clock he came into the house, still nebulous, and as he passed the open door of the library he heard a man's voice, not his father's.

"To me," said this voice, "the finest lines in all literature are those in Tennyson's 'Maud'—

"'Had it lain for a century dead,
My dust would hear her and beat,
And blossom in purple and red,
There somewhere around near her feet.'

"I think I have quoted correctly," continued the voice nervously, "but, at any rate, what I wished to

—ah—say was that I often think of those—ah— words; but I never think of them without thinking of—of—of *you*. I—ah——"

The nervous voice paused, and Penrod took an oblique survey of the room, himself unobserved. Margaret was seated in an easy chair and her face was turned away from Penrod, so that her expression of the moment remained unknown to him. Facing her, and leaning toward her with perceptible emotion, was Mr. Claude Blakely—a young man with whom Penrod had no acquaintance, though he had seen him, was aware of his identity, and had heard speech between Mrs. Schofield and Margaret which indicated that Mr. Blakely had formed the habit of calling frequently at the house. This was a brilliantly handsome young man; indeed, his face was so beautiful that even Penrod was able to perceive something about it which might be explicably pleasing—at least to women. And Penrod remembered that, on the last evening before Mr. Robert Williams's departure for college, Margaret had been peevish because Penrod had genially spent the greater portion of the evening with Robert and herself upon the porch. Margaret made it clear, later, that she strongly preferred to conduct her conversations

with friends unassisted—and as Penrod listened to
the faltering words of Mr. Claude Blakely, he felt
instinctively that, in a certain contingency, Margaret's indignation would be even more severe to-day
than on the former occasion.

Mr. Blakely coughed faintly and was able to continue.

"I mean to say that when I say that what Tennyson says—ah—seems to—to apply to—to a feeling
about you——"

At this point, finding too little breath in himself
to proceed, in spite of the fact that he had spoken
in an almost inaudible tone, Mr. Blakely stopped
again.

Something about this little scene was making a
deep impression upon Penrod. What that impression was, he could not possibly have stated; but he
had a sense of the imminence of a tender crisis, and
he perceived that the piquancy of affairs in the
library had reached a point which would brand an
intentional interruption as the act of a cold-blooded
ruffian. Suddenly it was as though a strong light
shone upon him: he decided that it was Mr. Blakely
who had told Margaret that her eyes were like blue
stars in heaven—*this* was the person who had caused

the hateful letter to be written! That decided
Penrod; his inspiration, so long waited for, had
come.

"I—I feel that perhaps I am not plain," said Mr.
Blakely, and immediately became red, whereas he
had been pale.   He was at least modest enough about
his looks to fear that Margaret might think he had
referred to them.   "I mean, not plain in another
sense—that is, I mean not that *I* am not plain in
saying what I mean to you—I mean, what you mean
to *me !*   I feel——"

This was the moment selected by Penrod.   He
walked carelessly into the library, inquiring in a loud,
bluff voice:

"Has anybody seen my dog around here anywheres?"

Mr. Blakely had inclined himself so far toward
Margaret, and he was sitting so near the edge of the
chair, that only a really wonderful bit of instinctive
gymnastics landed him upon his feet instead of upon his
back.   As for Margaret, she said, "Good gracious!"
and regarded Penrod blankly.

"Well," said Penrod breezily, "I guess it's no use
lookin' for him—he isn't anywheres around.   I guess
I'll sit down."   Herewith, he sank into an easy

chair, and remarked, as in comfortable explanation, "I'm kind of tired standin' up, anyway."

Even in this crisis, Margaret was a credit to her mother's training.

"Penrod, have you met Mr. Blakely?"

"What?"

Margaret primly performed the rite.

"Mr. Blakely, this is my little brother Penrod."

Mr. Blakely was understood to murmur, "How d'ye do?"

"I'm well," said Penrod.

Margaret bent a perplexed gaze upon him, and he saw that she had not divined his intentions, though the expression of Mr. Blakely was already beginning to be a little compensation for the ammonia outrage. Then, as the protracted silence which followed the introduction began to be a severe strain upon all parties, Penrod felt called upon to relieve it.

"I didn't have anything much to do this afternoon, anyway," he said. And at that there leaped a spark in Margaret's eye; her expression became severe.

"You should have gone to Sunday-school," she told him crisply.

"Well, I didn't!" said Penrod, with a bitterness so significant of sufferings connected with religion, ammonia, and herself, that Margaret, after giving him a thoughtful look, concluded not to urge the point.

Mr. Blakely smiled pleasantly. "I was looking out of the window a minute ago," he said, "and I saw a dog run across the street and turn the corner."

"What kind of a lookin' dog was it?" Penrod inquired, with languor.

"Well," said Mr. Blakely, "it was a—it was a nice-looking dog."

"What colour was he?"

"He was—ah—white. That is, I think——"

"It wasn't Duke," said Penrod. "Duke's kind of brownish-gray-like."

Mr. Blakely brightened.

"Yes, that was it," he said. "This dog I saw first had another dog with him—a brownish-gray dog."

"Little or big?" Penrod asked, without interest.

"Why, Duke's a little dog!" Margaret intervened. "Of *course*, if it was little, it must have been Duke."

"It *was* little," said Mr. Blakely too enthusiastically. "It was a little bit of a dog. I noticed it because it was so little."

"Couldn't 'a' been Duke, then," said Penrod. "Duke's a kind of a middle-sized dog." He yawned, and added: "I don't want him now. I want to stay in the house this afternoon, anyway. And it's better for Duke to be out in the fresh air."

Mr. Blakely coughed again and sat down, finding little to say. It was evident, also, that Margaret shared his perplexity; and another silence became so embarrassing that Penrod broke it.

"I was out in the sawdust-box," he said, "but it got kind of chilly." Neither of his auditors felt called upon to offer any comment, and presently he added, "I thought I better come in here where it's warmer."

"It's too warm," said Margaret, at once. "Mr. Blakely, would you mind opening a window?"

"By all means!" the young man responded earnestly, as he rose. "Maybe I'd better open two?"

"Yes," said Margaret; "that would be much better."

But Penrod watched Mr. Blakely open two windows to their widest, and betrayed no anxiety. His remarks upon the relative temperatures of the sawdust-box and the library had been made merely for the sake of creating sound in a silent place. When the windows had been open for several minutes, Penrod's placidity, though gloomy, denoted anything but discomfort from the draft, which was powerful, the day being windy.

It was Mr. Blakely's turn to break a silence, and he did it so unexpectedly that Margaret started. He sneezed.

"Perhaps——" Margaret began, but paused apprehensively. "Perhaps-per-per——" Her apprehensions became more and more poignant; her eyes seemed fixed upon some incredible disaster; she appeared to inflate while the catastrophe she foresaw became more and more imminent. All at once she collapsed, but the power decorum had over her was attested by the mildness of her sneeze after so threatening a prelude.

"Perhaps I'd better put one of the windows down," Mr. Blakely suggested.

"Both, I believe," said Margaret. "The room has cooled off, now, I think."

Mr. Blakely closed the windows, and, returning to a chair near Margaret, did his share in the production of another long period of quiet. Penrod allowed this one to pass without any vocal disturbance on his part. It may be, however, that his gaze was disturbing to Mr. Blakely, upon whose person it was glassily fixed with a self-forgetfulness that was almost morbid.

"Didn't you enjoy the last meeting of the Cotillion Club?" Margaret said finally.

And upon Mr. Blakely's answering absently in the affirmative, she suddenly began to be talkative. He seemed to catch a meaning in her fluency, and followed her lead, a conversation ensuing which at first had all the outward signs of eagerness. They talked with warm interest of people and events unknown to Penrod; they laughed enthusiastically about things beyond his ken; they appeared to have arranged a perfect way to enjoy themselves, no matter whether he was with them or elsewhere—but presently their briskness began to slacken; the appearance of interest became perfunctory. Within ten minutes the few last scattering semblances of gayety had passed, and they lapsed into the longest and most profound of all their silences indoors that day. Its.effect upon Penrod was to make him yawn and settle himself in his chair.

Then Mr. Blakely, coming to the surface out of deep inward communings, snapped his finger against the palm of his hand impulsively.

"By George!" he exclaimed, under his breath.

"What is it?" Margaret asked. "Did you remember something?"

"No, it's nothing," he said. "Nothing at all. But, by the way, it seems a pity for you to be missing the fine weather. I wonder if I could persuade you to take a little walk?"

Margaret, somewhat to the surprise of both the gentlemen present, looked uncertain.

"I don't know——" she said.

Mr. Blakely saw that she missed his point.

"One can talk better in the open, don't you think?" he urged, with a significant glance toward Penrod.

Margaret also glanced keenly at Penrod. "Well, perhaps." And then, "I'll get my hat," she said.

Penrod was on his feet before she left the room. He stretched himself.

"I'll get mine, too," he said.

But he carefully went to find it in a direction different from that taken by his sister, and he joined her and her escort not till they were at the front door, whither Mr. Blakely—with a last flickering of hope—had urged a flight in haste.

"I been thinkin' of takin' a walk, all afternoon,"

said Penrod pompously. "Don't matter to me which way we go."

The exquisite oval of Mr. Claude Blakely's face merged into outlines more rugged than usual; the conformation of his jaw became perceptible, and it could be seen that he had conceived an idea which was crystallizing into a determination.

"I believe it happens that this is our first walk together," he said to Margaret, as they reached the pavement, "but, from the kind of tennis you play, I judge that you could go a pretty good gait. Do you like walking fast?"

She nodded. "For exercise."

"Shall we try it then?"

"You set the pace," said Margaret. "I think I can keep up."

He took her at her word, and the amazing briskness of their start seemed a little sinister to Penrod, though he was convinced that he could do anything that Margaret could do, and also that neither she nor her comely friend could sustain such a speed for long. On the contrary, they actually increased it with each fleeting block they covered.

"Here!" he panted, when they had thus put something more than a half-mile behind them. "There

isn't anybody has to have a doctor, I guess!   What's
the use our walkin' so fast?"

In truth, Penrod was not walking, for his shorter
legs permitted no actual walking at such a speed;
his gait was a half-trot.

"Oh, *we're* out for a *walk!*" Mr. Blakely returned,
a note of gayety beginning to sound in his voice.
"Marg—ah—Miss Schofield, keep your head up and
breathe through your nose.   That's it!   You'll find
I was right in suggesting this.   It's going to
turn out gloriously!   Now, let's make it a little
faster."

Margaret murmured inarticulately, for she would
not waste her breath in a more coherent reply.   Her
cheeks were flushed; her eyes were brimming with
the wind, but when she looked at Penrod, they were
brimming with something more.   Gurgling sounds
came from her.

Penrod's expression had become grim.   He offered no second protest, mainly because he, likewise,
would not waste his breath, and if he would, he could
not.   Of breath in the ordinary sense—breath,
breathed automatically—he had none.   He had only
gasps to feed his straining lungs, and his half-trot,
which had long since become a trot, was changed for

a lope when Mr. Blakely reached his own best burst of speed.

And now people stared at the flying three. The gait of Margaret and Mr. Blakely could be called a walk only by courtesy, while Penrod's was becoming a kind of blind scamper. At times he zigzagged; other times, he fell behind, wabbling. Anon, with elbows flopping and his face sculptured like an antique mask, he would actually forge ahead, and then carom from one to the other of his companions as he fell back again.

Thus the trio sped through the coming of autumn dusk, outflying the fallen leaves that tumbled upon the wind. And still Penrod held to the task that he had set himself. The street lamps flickered into life, but on and on Claude Blakely led the lady, and on and on reeled the grim Penrod. Never once was he so far from them that they could have exchanged a word unchaperoned by his throbbing ear.

"*Oh!*" Margaret cried, and, halting suddenly, she draped herself about a lamp-post like a strip of bunting. "Guh-uh-guh-*goodness!*" she sobbed.

Penrod immediately drooped to the curb-stone, which he reached, by pure fortune, in a sitting position. Mr. Blakely leaned against a fence, and said

nothing, though his breathing was eloquent. "We—
we must go—go home," Margaret gasped. "We
must, if—if we can drag ourselves!"

Then Penrod showed them what mettle they had
tried to crack. A paroxysm of coughing shook him;
he spoke through it sobbingly:

"'Drag!' 'S jus' lul-like a girl! Ha-why I walk—
oof!—faster'n that every day—on my—way to
school." He managed to subjugate a tendency to
nausea. "What you—want to go—home for?" he
said. "Le's go on!"

In the darkness Mr. Claude Blakely's expression
could not be seen, nor was his voice heard. For
these and other reasons, his opinions and sentiments
may not be stated.

.   .   .   Mrs. Schofield was looking rather anxiously forth from her front door when the two adult
figures and the faithful smaller one came up the walk.

"I was getting uneasy," she said. "Papa and I
came in and found the house empty. It's after
seven. Oh, Mr. Blakely, is that you?"

"Good-evening," he said. "I fear I must be
keeping an engagement. Good-night. Good-night,
Miss Schofield."

"Good-night."

"Well, good-night," Penrod called, staring after him. But Mr. Blakely was already too far away to hear him, and a moment later Penrod followed his mother and sister into the house.

"I let Della go to church," Mrs. Schofield said to Margaret. "You and I might help Katie get supper."

"Not for a few minutes," Margaret returned gravely, looking at Penrod. "Come upstairs, mamma; I want to tell you something."

Penrod cackled hoarse triumph and defiance.

"Go on! Tell! What *I* care? You try to poison a person in church again, and then laugh in his face, you'll see what you get!"

But after his mother had retired with Margaret to the latter's room, he began to feel disturbed in spite of his firm belief that his cause was wholly that of justice victorious. Margaret had insidious ways of stating a case; and her point of view, no matter how absurd or unjust, was almost always adopted by Mr. and Mrs. Schofield in cases of controversy.

Penrod became uneasy. Perceiving himself to be in danger, he decided that certain measures were warranted. Unquestionably, it would be well to know beforehand in what terms Margaret would couch the charges which he supposed he must face in open court—that is to say, at the supper-table. He stole softly up the stairs, and, flattening himself against the wall, approached Margaret's door, which was about an inch ajar.

He heard his mother making sounds which appalled him—he took them for sobs. And then Margaret's voice rang out in a peal of insane laughter. Trembling, he crept nearer the door. Within the room Margaret was clinging to her mother, and both were trying to control their hilarity.

"He did it all to get even!" Margaret exclaimed, wiping her eyes. "He came in at just the right time. That *goose* was beginning to talk his silly, soft talk—the way he does with every girl in town—and he was almost proposing, and I didn't know how to stop him. And then Penrod came in and did it for me. I could have hugged Penrod, mamma, I actually could! And I saw he meant to stay to get even for that ammonia—and, oh, I worked so hard to make him think I wanted him to *go !* Mamma, mamma, if you could have *seen* that walk! That *goose* kept thinking he could wear Penrod out or drop him behind, but I knew he couldn't so long as Penrod believed he was worrying us and getting even. And that *goose* thought I *wanted* to get rid of Penrod, too; and the conceited thing said it would turn out 'gloriously,' meaning we'd be alone together pretty soon—I'd like to shake him! You see, I pretended so well, in order to make Penrod stick to us, that *goose* believed I meant it! And if he hadn't tried to walk Penrod off his legs, he wouldn't have wilted his own collar and worn himself out, and I think he'd have hung on until you'd have had to invite him to stay to supper, and he'd have stayed on all evening, and I wouldn't have had a chance to write to Robert Williams. Mamma, there have been lots of times when I haven't been thankful for Penrod, but to-day I could have got down on my knees to you and papa for giving me such a brother!"

In the darkness of the hall, as a small but crushed and broken form stole away from the crack in the door, a gigantic Eye seemed to form—seemed to glare down upon Penrod—warning him that the way of vengeance is the way of bafflement, and that genius may not prevail against the trickeries of women.

"This has been a *nice* day!" Penrod muttered hoarsely.

CHAPTER XVIII

ON ACCOUNT OF THE WEATHER

THERE is no boredom (not even an invalid's) comparable to that of a boy who has nothing to do. When a man says he has nothing to do, he speaks idly; there is always more than he can do. Grown women never say they have nothing to do, and when girls or little girls say they have nothing to do, they are merely airing an affectation. But when a boy has nothing to do, he has actually nothing at all to do; his state is pathetic, and when he complains of it, his voice is haunting.

Mrs. Schofield was troubled by this uncomfortable quality in the voice of her son, who came to her thrice, in his search for entertainment or even employment, one Saturday afternoon during the February thaw. Few facts are better established than that the February thaw is the poorest time of year for everybody. But for a boy it is worse than poorest; it is bankrupt. The remnant streaks of old soot-speckled snow left against the north walls

of houses have no power to inspire; rather, they
are dreary reminders of sports long since carried to
satiety.   One cares little even to eat such snow, and
the eating of icicles, also, has come to be a flaccid and
stale diversion.   There is no ice to bear a skate;
there is only a vast sufficiency of cold mud, practi-
cally useless.   Sunshine flickers shiftily, coming and
going without any honest purpose; snow-squalls
blow for five minutes, the flakes disappearing as
they touch the earth; half an hour later rain sputters,
turns to snow, and then turns back to rain—and the
sun disingenuously beams out again, only to be shut
off like a rogue's lantern.   And all the wretched
while, if a boy sets foot out of doors, he must be
harassed about his overcoat and rubbers; he is
warned against tracking up the plastic lawn and
sharply advised to stay inside the house.   Saturday
might as well be Sunday.

Thus the season.   Penrod had sought all possible
means to pass the time.   A full half-hour of vehement yodelling in the Williams's yard had failed to
bring forth comrade Sam; and at last a coloured
woman had opened a window to inform Penrod
that her intellect was being unseated by his vocalizations, which surpassed in unpleasantness, she

claimed, every sound in her previous experience—
and, for the sake of definiteness, she stated her age
to be fifty-three years and four months. She added
that all members of the Williams family had gone
out of town to attend the funeral of a relative, but
she wished that they might have remained to attend
Penrod's, which she confidently predicted as imminent if the neighbourhood followed its natural
impulse.

Penrod listened for a time, but departed before
the conclusion of the oration. He sought other
comrades, with no success; he even went to the
length of yodelling in the yard of that best of boys,
Georgie Bassett. Here was failure again, for Georgie
signalled to him, through a closed window, that a
closeting with dramatic literature was preferable to
the society of a playmate; and the book which
Georgie exhibited was openly labelled, "300 Choice
Declamations." Georgie also managed to convey
another reason for his refusal of Penrod's companion-
ship, the visitor being conversant with lip-reading
through his studies at the "movies."

"*Too muddy!*"

Penrod went home.

"Well," said Mrs. Schofield, having almost exhausted a mother's powers of suggestion, "well, why don't you give Duke a bath?" She was that far depleted when Penrod came to her the third time.

Mothers' suggestions are wonderful for little children but sometimes lack lustre when a boy is about twelve—an age to which the ideas of a Swede farm-hand would usually prove more congenial. However, the dim and melancholy eye of Penrod showed a pale gleam, and he departed. He gave Duke a bath.

The entertainment proved damp and discouraging for both parties. Duke began to tremble even before he was lifted into the water, and after his first immersion he was revealed to be a dog weighing about one-fourth of what an observer of Duke, when Duke was dry, must have guessed his weight to be. His wetness and the disclosure of his extreme fleshly insignificance appeared to mortify him profoundly. He wept. But, presently, under Penrod's thorough ministrations—for the young master was inclined to make this bath last as long as possible— Duke plucked up a heart and began a series of passionate attempts to close the interview. As this was his first bath since September, the effects were lavish and impressionistic, both upon Penrod and upon the bathroom. However, the imperious boy's loud remonstrances contributed to bring about the result desired by Duke.

Mrs. Schofield came running, and eloquently put an end to Duke's winter bath. When she had suggested this cleansing as a pleasant means of passing the time, she assumed that it would take place in a washtub in the cellar; and Penrod's location of the performance in her own bathroom was far from her intention.

Penrod found her language oppressive, and, having been denied the right to rub Duke dry with a bath-towel—or even with the cover of a table in the next room—the dismal boy, accompanied by his dismal dog, set forth, by way of the kitchen door, into the dismal weather. With no purpose in mind, they mechanically went out to the alley, where Penrod leaned morosely against the fence, and Duke stood shivering close by, his figure still emaciated and his tail absolutely withdrawn from view.

There was a cold, wet wind, however; and before long Duke found his condition unendurable. He was past middle age and cared little for exercise, but he saw that something must be done. Therefore,

he made a vigorous attempt to dry himself in a
dog's way. Throwing himself, shoulders first,
upon the alley mud, he slid upon it, back downward;
he rolled and rolled and rolled. He began to feel
lively and rolled the more; in every way he convinced
Penrod that dogs have no regard for appearances.
Also, having discovered an ex-fish near the Herman
and Verman cottage, Duke confirmed an impression of Penrod's that dogs have a peculiar fancy in
the matter of odours which they like to wear.

Growing livelier and livelier, Duke now wished to
play with his master. Penrod was anything but
fastidious; nevertheless, under the circumstances,
he withdrew to the kitchen, leaving Duke to play
by himself, outside.

Della, the cook, was comfortably making rolls
and entertaining a caller with a cup of tea. Penrod
lingered a few moments, but found even his attention to the conversation ill received, while his attempts to take part in it met outright rebuff. His
feelings were hurt; he passed broodingly to the front
part of the house, and flung himself wearily into an
armchair in the library. With glazed eyes he stared
at shelves of books that meant to him just what
the wall-paper meant, and he sighed from the

abyss. His legs tossed and his arms flopped; he got up, scratched himself exhaustively, and shuffled to a window. Ten desolate minutes he stood there, gazing out sluggishly upon a soggy world. During this time two wet delivery-wagons and four elderly women under umbrellas were all that crossed his field of vision. Somewhere in the world, he thought, there was probably a boy who lived across the street from a jail or a fire-engine house, and had windows worth looking out of. Penrod rubbed his nose up and down the pane slowly, continuously, and without the slightest pleasure; and he again scratched himself wherever it was possible to do so, though he did not even itch. There was nothing in his life.

Such boredom as he was suffering can become agony, and an imaginative creature may do wild things to escape it; many a grown person has taken to drink on account of less pressure than was upon Penrod during that intolerable Saturday.

A faint sound in his ear informed him that Della, in the kitchen, had uttered a loud exclamation, and he decided to go back there. However, since his former visit had resulted in a rebuff that still rankled, he paused outside the kitchen door, which was

slightly ajar, and listened. He did this idly, and
with no hope of hearing anything interesting or
helpful.

"Snakes!" Della exclaimed. "Didja say the poor
man was seein' snakes, Mrs. Cullen?"

"No, Della," Mrs Cullen returned dolorously;
"jist one. Flora says he niver see more th'n one—
jist one big, long, ugly-faced horr'ble black one; the
same one comin' back an' makin' a fizzin' n'ise at
um iv'ry time he had the fit on um. 'Twas alw'ys
the same snake; an' he'd holler at Flora. 'Here it
comes ag'in, *oh*, me soul!' he'd holler. 'The big,
black, ugly-faced thing; it's as long as the front
fence!' he'd holler, 'an' it's makin' a fizzin' n'ise at
me, an' breathin' in me face!' he'd holler. 'Fer th'
love o' hivin', Flora,' he'd holler, 'it's got a little
black man wit' a gassly white forehead a-pokin' of
it along wit' a broom-handle, an' a-sickin' it on me,
the same as a boy sicks a dog on a poor cat. Fer
the love o' hivin', Flora,' he'd holler, 'cantcha fright
it away from me before I go out o' me head?'"

"Poor Tom!" said Della with deep compassion.
"An' the poor man out of his head all the time, an'
not knowin' it! 'Twas awful fer Flora to sit there
an' hear such things in the night like that!"

"You may believe yerself whin ye say it!" Mrs. Cullen agreed. "Right the very night the poor soul died, he was hollerin' how the big black snake and the little black man wit' the gassly white forehead a-pokin' it wit' a broomstick had come fer um. 'Fright 'em away, Flora!' he was croakin', in a v'ice that hoarse an' husky 'twas hard to make out what he says. 'Fright 'em away, Flora!' he says. ''Tis the big, black, ugly-faced snake, as black as a black stockin' an' thicker round than me leg at the thigh before I was wasted away!' he says, poor man. 'It's makin' the fizzin' n'ise awful to-night,' he says. 'An' the little black man wit' the gassly white forehead is a-laughin',' he says. 'He's a-laughin' an' a-pokin' the big, black, fizzin,' ugly-faced snake wit' his broomstick——' "

Della was unable to endure the description.

"Don't tell me no more, Mrs. Cullen!" she protested. "Poor Tom! I thought Flora was wrong last week whin she hid the whisky. 'Twas takin' it away from him that killed him—an' him already so sick!"

"Well," said Mrs. Cullen, "he hardly had the strengt' to drink much, she tells me, after he see the big snake an' the little black divil the first time.

Poor woman, she says he talked so plain she sees 'em both herself, iv'ry time she looks at the poor body where it's laid out. She says——"

"Don't tell me!" cried the impressionable Della. "Don't tell me, Mrs. Cullen! I can most see 'em meself, right here in me own kitchen! Poor Tom! To think whin I bought me new hat, only last week, the first time I'd be wearin' it'd be to his funeral. To-morrow afternoon, it is?"

"At two o'clock," said Mrs. Cullen. "Ye'll be comin' to th' house to-night, o' course, Della?"

"I will," said Della. "After what I've been hearin' from ye, I'm most afraid to come, but I'll do it. Poor Tom! I remember the day him an' Flora was married——"

But the eavesdropper heard no more; he was on his way up the back stairs. Life and light—and purpose—had come to his face once more.

Margaret was out for the afternoon. Unostentatiously, he went to her room, and for the next few minutes occupied himself busily therein. He was so quiet that his mother, sewing in her own room, would not have heard him except for the obstinacy of one of the drawers in Margaret's bureau. Mrs. Schofield went to the door of her daughter's room.

"What are you doing, Penrod?"

"Nothin'."

"You're not disturbing any of Margaret's things, are you?"

"No, ma'am," said the meek lad.

"What did you jerk that drawer open for?"

"Ma'am?"

"You heard me, Penrod."

"Yes, ma'am. I was just lookin' for sumpthing."

"For what?" Mrs Schofield asked. "You know that nothing of yours would be in Margaret's room, Penrod, don't you?"

"Ma'am?"

"What was it you wanted?" she asked, rather impatiently.

"I was just lookin' for some pins."

"Very well," she said, and handed him two from the shoulder of her blouse.

"I ought to have more," he said. "I want about forty."

"What for?"

"I just want to *make* sumpthing, mamma," he said plaintively. "My goodness! Can't I even want to have a few pins without everybody makin' such a fuss about it you'd think I was doin' a srime!"

"Doing a what, Penrod?"

"A *srime!*" he repeated, with emphasis; and a moment's reflection enlightened his mother.

"Oh, a crime!" she exclaimed. "You *must* quit reading the murder trials in the newspapers, Penrod. And when you read words you don't know how to pronounce you ought to ask either your papa or me."

"Well, I am askin' you about sumpthing now," said Penrod. "Can't I even have a few *pins* without stoppin' to talk about everything in the newspapers, mamma?"

"Yes," she said, laughing at his seriousness; and she took him to her room, and bestowed upon him five or six rows torn from a paper of pins. "That ought to be plenty," she said, "whatever you want to make."

And she smiled after his retreating figure, not noting that he looked softly bulky around the body, and held his elbows unnaturally tight to his sides. She was assured of the innocence of anything to be made with pins, and forebore to press investigation. For Penrod to be playing with pins seemed almost girlish. Unhappy woman, it pleased her to have her son seem girlish!

Penrod went out to the stable, tossed his pins into

the wheelbarrow, then took from his pocket and unfolded six pairs of long black stockings, indubitably the property of his sister. (Evidently Mrs. Schofield had been a little late in making her appearance at the door of Margaret's room.)

Penrod worked systematically; he hung the twelve stockings over the sides of the wheelbarrow, and placed the wheelbarrow beside a large packing-box which was half full of excelsior. One after another, he stuffed the stockings with excelsior, till they looked like twelve long black sausages. Then he pinned the top of one stocking securely over the stuffed foot of another, pinning the top of a third to the foot of the second, the top of a fourth to the foot of the third—and continued operations in this fashion until the twelve stockings were the semblance of one long and sinuous black body, sufficiently suggestive to any normal eye.

He tied a string to one end of this unpleasant-looking thing, led it around the stable, and, by vigorous manipulations, succeeded in making it wriggle realistically; but he was not satisfied, and, dropping the string listlessly, sat down in the wheelbarrow to ponder. Penrod sometimes proved that there were within him the makings of an artist;

he had become fascinated by an idea, and could not be content until that idea was beautifully realized.   He had meant to create a big, long, ugly-faced horrible black snake with which to interest Della and her friend, Mrs. Cullen; but he felt that results, so far, were too crude for exploitation.   Merely to lead the pinned stockings by a string was little to fulfill his ambitious vision.

Finally, he rose from the wheelbarrow.

"If I only had a cat!" he said dreamily.

CHAPTER XIX

CREATIVE ART

HE WENT forth, seeking.

The Schofield household was catless this winter, but there was a nice white cat at he Williams'. Penrod strolled thoughtfully over to he Williams' yard.

He was entirely successful, not even having been een by the sensitive coloured woman, aged fifty-hree years and four months.

But still Penrod was thoughtful. The artist within im was unsatisfied with his materials: and upon his eturn to the stable he placed the cat beneath an verturned box, and once more sat down in the nspiring wheelbarrow, pondering. His expression, oncentrated and yet a little anxious, was like that f a painter at work upon a portrait which may or nay not turn out to be a masterpiece. The cat did ot disturb him by her purring, though she was, in-leed, already purring. She was one of those cozy, oungish cats—plump, even a little full-bodied, perhaps, and rather conscious of the figure—that are entirely conventional and domestic by nature, and will set up a ladylike housekeeping anywhere without making a fuss about it. If there were a fault in these cats, overcomplacency might be the name for it; they are a shade too sure of themselves, and their assumption that the world means to treat them respectfully has just a little taint of the *grande dame*. Consequently, they are liable to great outbreaks of nervous energy from within, engendered by the extreme surprises which life sometimes holds in store for them. They lack the pessimistic imagination.

Mrs. Williams' cat was content upon a strange floor and in the confining enclosure of a strange box. She purred for a time, then trustfully fell asleep. 'Twas well she slumbered; she would need all her powers presently.

She slumbered, and dreamed not that she would wake to mingle with events which were to alter her serene disposition radically, and cause her to become hasty-tempered and abnormally suspicious for the rest of her life.

Meanwhile, Penrod appeared to reach a doubtful solution of his problem. His expression was still somewhat clouded as he brought from the storeroom ɔf the stable a small fragment of a broken mirror, two ɔaint brushes, and two old cans, one containing ɔlack paint and the other white. He regarded himself earnestly in the mirror; then, with some reluctance, he dipped a brush into one of the cans, and slowly painted his nose a midnight black. He was ɔn the point of spreading this decoration to cover the lower part of his face, when he paused, brush halfway between can and chin.

What arrested him was a sound from the alley—a sound of drumming upon tin. The eyes of Penrod became significant of rushing thoughts; his expression cleared and brightened. He ran to the alley doors and flung them open.

"Oh, Verman!" he shouted.

Marching up and down before the cottage across the alley, Verman plainly considered himself to be an army. Hanging from his shoulders by a string was an old tin wash-basin, whereon he beat cheerily with two dry bones, once the chief supports of a chicken. Thus he assuaged his *ennui*.

"Verman, come on in here," Penrod called. "I got sumpthing for you to do you'll like awful well."

Verman halted, ceased to drum, and stared. His gaze was not fixed particularly upon Penrod's nose, however, and neither now nor later did he make any remark or gesture referring to this casual eccentricity. He expected things like that upon Penrod or Sam Williams. And as for Penrod himself, he had already forgotten that his nose was painted.

"Come on, Verman!"

Verman continued to stare, not moving. He had received such invitations before, and they had not always resulted to his advantage. Within that stable things had happened to him the like of which he was anxious to avoid in the future.

"Oh, come ahead, Verman!" Penrod urged, and, divining logic in the reluctance confronting him, he added, "This ain't goin' to be anything like last time, Verman. I got sumpthing just *splendud* for you to do!"

Verman's expression hardened; he shook his head decisively.

"Mo," he said.

"Oh, *come* on, Verman?" Penrod pleaded. "It isn't anything goin' to *hurt* you, is it? I tell you it's sumpthing you'd give a good deal to *get* to do, if you knew what it is."

"Mo!" said Verman firmly. "I mome maw woo!"

Penrod offered arguments.

"Look, Verman!" he said. "Listen here a minute, an't you? How d'you know you don't want to ntil you know what it is? A person *can't* know they on't want to do a thing even before the other person ells 'em what they're goin' to get 'em to do, can hey? For all you know, this thing I'm goin' to get ou to do might be sumpthing you wouldn't miss oin' for anything there is! For all you know, Ver- 1an, it might be sumpthing like this: well, f'rin- tance, s'pose I was standin' here, and you were over 1ere, sort of like the way you are now, and I says, Iello, Verman!' and then I'd go on and tell you 1ere was sumpthing I was goin' to get you to do; and ou'd say you wouldn't do it, even before you heard hat it was, why where'd be any sense to *that?* For ll you know, I might of been goin' to get you to eat five-cent bag o' peanuts."

Verman had listened obdurately until he heard the 1st few words, but as they fell upon his ear, he re- 1xed, and advanced to the stable doors, smiling and xtending his open right hand.

"Aw wi'," he said. "Gi'm here."

"Well," Penrod returned, a trifle embarrassed, I didn't say it *was* peanuts, did I? Honest, Ver- 1an, it's sumpthing you'll like better'n a few old

peanuts that most of 'em'd prob'ly have worms in
'em, anyway. All I want you to do is——"

But Verman was not favourably impressed; his
face hardened again.

"Mo!" he said, and prepared to depart.

"Look here, Verman," Penrod urged. "It isn't
goin' to hurt you just to come in here and see what
I got for you, is it? You can do *that* much, can't
you?"

Surely such an appeal must have appeared reasonable, even to Verman, especially since its effect was
aided by the promising words, "See what I got for
you." Certainly Verman yielded to it, though perhaps a little suspiciously. He advanced a few cautious steps into the stable.

"Look!" Penrod cried, and he ran to the stuffed
and linked stockings, seized the leading-string, and
vigorously illustrated his further remarks. "How's
that for a big, long, ugly-faced horr'ble black ole
snake, Verman? Look at her follow me all round
anywhere I feel like goin'! Look at her wiggle, will
you, though? Look how I make her do anything I
tell her to. Lay down, you ole snake, you! See her
lay down when I tell her to, Verman? Wiggle,
you ole snake, you! See her wiggle, Verman?"

"Hi!" Undoubtedly Verman felt some pleasure.

"Now, listen, Verman!" Penrod continued, hastening to make the most of the opportunity. "Listen! I fixed up this good ole snake just for you. I'm goin' to give her to you."

"*Hi!*"

On account of a previous experience not unconnected with cats, and likely to prejudice Verman, Penrod decided to postpone mentioning Mrs. Williams' pet until he should have secured Verman's coöperation in the enterprise irretrievably.

"All you got to do," he went on, "is to chase this good ole snake around, and sort o' laugh and keep pokin' it with the handle o' that rake yonder. I'm goin' to saw it off just so's you can poke your good ole snake with it, Verman."

"Aw wi'," said Verman, and extending his open hand again, he uttered a hopeful request.

"Peamup?"

His host perceived that Verman had misunderstood him. "Peanuts!" he exclaimed. "My goodness! I didn't say I *had* any peanuts, did I? I only said s'pose f'rinstance I *did* have some. My goodness! You don't expeck me to go round here all day workin' like a dog to make a good ole snake for you and then give you a bag o' peanuts to hire you to *play* with it, do you, Verman? My goodness!"

Verman's hand fell, with a little disappointment.

"Aw wi'," he said, consenting to accept the snake without the bonus.

"That's the boy! *Now* we're all right, Verman; and pretty soon I'm goin' to saw that rake-handle off for you, too; so's you can kind o' guide your good ole snake around with it; but first—well, first there's just one more thing's got to be done. I'll show you— it won't take but a minute." Then, while Verman watched him wonderingly, he went to the can of white paint and dipped a brush therein. "It won't get on your clo'es much, or anything, Verman," he explained. "I only just got to——"

But as he approached, dripping brush in hand, the wondering look was all gone from Verman; determination took its place.

"Mo!" he said, turned his back, and started for outdoors.

"Look here, Verman," Penrod cried. "I haven't done anything to you yet, have I? It isn't goin' to hurt you, is it? You act like a little teeny bit o' paint was goin' to kill you! What's the matter of you? I only just got to paint the top part of your

face; I'm not goin' to *touch* the other part of it—nor
your hands or anything. All *I* want——"

"*Mo!*" said Verman from the doorway.

"Oh, my goodness!" moaned Penrod; and in desperation he drew forth from his pocket his entire
fortune. "All right, Verman," he said resignedly.
"If you won't do it any other way, here's a nickel,
and you can go and buy you some peanuts when we
get through. But if I give you this money, you got
to promise to wait till we *are* through, and you
got to promise to do anything I tell you to. You
goin' to promise?"

The eyes of Verman glistened; he returned, gave
bond, and, grasping the coin, burst into the rich
laughter of a gourmand.

Penrod immediately painted him dead white above
the eyes, all round his head and including his hair.
It took all the paint in the can.

Then the artist mentioned the presence of Mrs.
Williams' cat, explained in full his ideas concerning
the docile animal, and the long black snake, and
Della and her friend, Mrs. Cullen, while Verman
listened with anxiety, but remained true to his oath.

They removed the stocking at the end of the long
black snake, and cut four holes in the foot and ankle

of it. They removed the excelsior, placed Mrs. Williams' cat in the stocking, shook her down into the
lower section of it; drew her feet through the four
holes there, leaving her head in the toe of the stocking; then packed the excelsior down on top of her,
and once more attached the stocking to the rest of
the long, black snake.

How shameful is the ease of the historian! He
sits in his dressing-gown to write: "The enemy at-
tacked in force——" The tranquil pen, moving in a
cloud of tobacco smoke, leaves upon the page its
little hieroglyphics, serenely summing up the monstrous deeds and sufferings of men of action. How
cold, how niggardly, to state merely that Penrod and
the painted Verman succeeded in giving the long,
black snake a motive power, or tractor, apparently
its own but consisting of Mrs. Williams' cat!

She was drowsy when they lifted the box; she was
still drowsy when they introduced part of her into
the orifice of the stocking; but she woke to full,
vigorous young life when she perceived that their
purpose was for her to descend into the black depths
of that stocking head first.

Verman held the mouth of the stocking stretched,
and Penrod manipulated the cat; but she left her

hearty mark on both of them before, in a moment of unfortunate inspiration, she humped her back while she was upside down, and Penrod took advantage of the concavity to increase it even more than she desired. The next instant she was assisted downward into the gloomy interior, with excelsior already beginning to block the means of egress.

Gymnastic moments followed; there were times when both boys hurled themselves full-length upon the floor, seizing the animated stocking with far-extended hands; and even when the snake was a complete thing, with legs growing from its unquestionably ugly face, either Penrod or Verman must keep a grasp upon it, for it would not be soothed, and refused, over and over, to calm itself, even when addressed as, "Poor pussy!" and "Nice 'ittle kitty!"

Finally, they thought they had their good ole snake "about quieted down," as Penrod said, because the animated head had remained in one place for an unusual length of time, though the legs produced a rather sinister effect of crouching, and a noise like a distant planing-mill came from the interior—and then Duke appeared in the doorway.

He was still feeling lively.

CHAPTER XX

THE DEPARTING GUEST

B Y THE time Penrod returned from chasing
Duke to the next corner, Verman had the
long, black snake down from the rafter where
its active head had taken refuge, with the rest of it
dangling; and both boys agreed that Mrs. Williams'
cat must certainly be able to "see *some*, anyway,"
through the meshes of the stocking.

"Well," said Penrod, "it's gettin' pretty near
dark, what with all this bother and mess we been
havin' around here, and I expeck as soon as I get
this good ole broom-handle fixed out of the rake for
you, Verman, it'll be about time to begin what we
had to go and take all this trouble *for*."

. . . . Mr. Schofield had brought an old
friend home to dinner with him: "Dear old Joe
Gilling," he called this friend when introducing him
to Mrs. Schofield. Mr. Gilling, as Mrs. Schofield
was already informed by telephone, had just hap-

pened to turn up in town that day, and had called
on his classmate at the latter's office. The two
had not seen each other in eighteen years.

Mr. Gilling was a tall man, clad highly in the
mode, and brought to a polished and powdered finish
by barber and manicurist; but his colour was peculiar, being almost unhumanly florid, and, as Mrs.
Schofield afterward claimed to have noticed, his
eyes "wore a nervous, apprehensive look," his hands
were tremulous, and his manner was "queer and
jerky"—at least, that is how she defined it.

She was not surprised to hear him state that he
was travelling for his health and not upon business.
He had not been really well for several years, he
said.

At that, Mr. Schofield laughed and slapped him
heartily on the back.

"Oh, mercy!" cried Mr. Gilling, leaping in his
chair. "What *is* the matter?"

"Nothing!" Mr. Schofield laughed. "I just
slapped you the way we used to slap each other on
the campus. What I was going to say was that you
have no business being a bachelor. With all your
money, and nothing to do but travel and sit around
hotels and clubs, no wonder you've grown bilious."

"Oh, no; I'm not bilious," said Mr. Gilling uncomfortably. "I'm not bilious at all."

"You ought to get married," Mr. Schofield returned. "You ought——" He paused, for Mr. Gilling had jumped again. "What's the trouble, Joe?"

"Nothing. I thought perhaps—perhaps you were going to slap me on the back again."

"Not this time," said Mr. Schofield, renewing his laughter. "Well, is dinner about ready?" he asked, turning to his wife. "Where are Margaret and Penrod?"

"Margaret's just come in," Mrs. Schofield answered. "She'll be down in a minute, and Penrod's around somewhere."

"Penrod?" Mr. Gilling repeated curiously, in his nervous, serious way. "What is Penrod?"

And at this Mrs. Schofield joined in her husband's laughter. Mr. Schofield explained.

"Penrod's our young son," he said. "He's not much for looks, maybe, but he's been pretty good lately, and sometimes we're almost inclined to be proud of him. You'll see him in a minute, old Joe!"

Old Joe saw him even sooner. Instantly, as Mr.

Schofield finished his little prediction, the most shocking uproar ever heard in that house burst forth in the kitchen. Distinctly Irish shrieks unlimited came from that quarter—together with the clashing of hurled metal and tin, the appealing sound of breaking china, and the hysterical barking of a dog.

The library door flew open, and Mrs. Cullen appeared as a mingled streak crossing the room from one door to the other. She was followed by a boy with a coal-black nose; and between his feet, as he entered, there appeared a big, long, black, horr'ble snake, with frantic legs springing from what appeared to be its head; and it further fulfilled Mrs. Cullen's description by making a fizzin' noise. Accompanying the snake, and still faithfully endeavouring to guide it with the detached handle of a rake, was a small black demon with a gassly white forehead and gasslier white hair. Duke, evidently still feeling his bath, was doing all in his power to aid the demon in making the snake step lively. A few kitchen implements followed this fugitive procession through the library doorway.

The long, black snake became involved with a leg of the heavy table in the centre of the room. The head developed spasms of agility; there were

clawings and rippings; then the foremost section of
the long, black snake detached itself, bounded into
the air, and, after turning a number of somersaults,
became, severally, a torn stocking, excelsior, and a
lunatic cat. The ears of this cat were laid .back
flat upon its head and its speed was excessive upon
a fairly circular track it laid out for itself in the
library. Flying round this orbit, it perceived the
open doorway; passed through it, thence to the
kitchen, and outward and onward—Della having
left the kitchen door open in her haste as she retired
to the backyard.

The black demon with the gassly white forehead
and hair, finding himself in the presence of grown
people who were white all over, turned in his tracks
and followed Mrs. Williams' cat to the great outdoors. Duke preceded Verman. Mrs. Cullen vanished. Of the apparition, only wreckage and a
rightfully apprehensive Penrod were left.

"But where—" Mrs. Schofield began, a few minutes later, looking suddenly mystified—"where—
where——"

"Where what?" asked Mr. Schofield testily.
"What are you talking about?" His nerves were

jarred, and he was rather hoarse after what he had been saying to Penrod. (That regretful necromancer was now upstairs doing unhelpful things to his nose over a washstand.) "What do you mean by, 'Where, where, where?'" Mr. Schofield demanded. "I don't see any sense to it."

"But where is your old classmate?" she cried. "Where's Mr. Gilling?"

She was the first to notice this striking absence.

"By George!" Mr. Schofield exclaimed. "Where *is* old Joe?"

Margaret intervened. "You mean that tall, pale man who was calling?" she asked.

"Pale, no!" said her father. "He's as flushed as——"

"He was pale when *I* saw him," said Margaret. "He had his hat and coat, and he was trying to get out of the front door when I came running downstairs. He couldn't work the catch for a minute, but before I got to the foot of the steps he managed to turn it and open the door. He went out before I could think what to say to him, he was in such a hurry. I guess everything was so confused you didn't notice—but he's certainly gone."

Mrs. Schofield turned to her husband.

"But I thought he was going to stay to dinner!" she cried.

Mr. Schofield shook his head, admitting himself floored. Later, having mentally gone over everything that might shed light on the curious behaviour of old Joe, he said, without preface:

"He wasn't at all dissipated when we were in college."

Mrs. Schofield nodded severely. "Maybe this was just the best thing could have happened to him, after all," she said.

"It may be," returned her husband. "I don't say it isn't. *But* that isn't going to make any difference in what I'm going to do to Penrod!"

CHAPTER XXI

YEARNINGS

THE next day a new ambition entered into Penrod Schofield; it was heralded by a flourish of trumpets and set up a great noise within his being.

On his way home from Sunday-school he had paused at a corner to listen to a brass band, which was returning from a funeral, playing a medley of airs from "The Merry Widow," and as the musicians came down the street, walking so gracefully, the sun picked out the gold braid upon their uniforms and splashed fire from their polished instruments. Penrod marked the shapes of the great bass horns, the suave sculpture of their brazen coils, and the grand, sensational flare of their mouths. And he saw plainly that these noble things, to be mastered, needed no more than some breath blown into them during the fingering of a few simple keys. Then obediently they gave forth those vast but dulcet sounds which stirred his spirit as no other sounds could stir it quite.

320

The leader of the band, walking ahead, was a pleasing figure, nothing more. Penrod supposed him to be a mere decoration, and had never sympathized with Sam Williams' deep feeling about drum-majors. The cornets, the trombones, the smaller horns were rather interesting, of course; and the drums had charm, especially the bass drum, which must be partially supported by a youth in front; but, immeasurably above all these, what fascinated Penrod was the little man with the monster horn. There Penrod's widening eyes remained transfixed—upon the horn, so dazzling, with its broad spaces of brassy high lights, and so overwhelming, with its mouth as wide as a tub, that there was something almost threatening about it.

The little, elderly band-musician walked manfully as he blew his great horn; and in that pompous engine of sound, the boy beheld a spectacle of huge forces under human control. To Penrod, the horn meant power, and the musician meant mastery over power, though, of course, Penrod did not know that this was how he really felt about the matter.

Grandiloquent sketches were passing and interchanging before his mind's eye—Penrod, in noble

aiment, marching down the staring street, his shoul-
ers swaying professionally, the roar of the horn he
ore submerging all other sounds; Penrod on horse-
ack, blowing the enormous horn and leading wild
ordes to battle, while Marjorie Jones looked on
rom the sidewalk; Penrod astounding his mother
nd father and sister by suddenly serenading them
ı the library. "Why, Penrod, where *did* you learn
ɔ play like this?"

These were vague and shimmering glories of vision
ather than definite plans for his life work, yet he
id with all his will determine to own and play upon
ɔme roaring instrument of brass. And, after all,
his was no new desire of his; it was only an old one
ıflamed to take a new form. Nor was music the
ɔot of it, for the identical desire is often uproarious
mong them that hate music. What stirred in
'enrod was new neither in him nor in the world,
ut old—old as old Adam, old as the childishness of
ıan. All children have it, of course: they are all
nxious to Make a Noise in the World.

While the band approached, Penrod marked the
ime with his feet; then he fell into step and accom-
anied the musicians down the street, keeping as
ear as possible to the little man with the big horn.

There were four or five other boys, strangers, also marching with the band, but these were light spirits, their flushed faces and prancing legs proving that they were merely in a state of emotional reaction to music. Penrod, on the contrary, was grave. He kept his eyes upon the big horn, and, now and then, he gave an imitation of it. His fingers moved upon invisible keys, his cheeks puffed out, and, from far down in his throat, he produced strange sounds: "Taw, p'taw-p'taw! Taw, p'taw-p'taw! PAW!"

The other boys turned back when the musicians ceased to play, but Penrod marched on, still keeping close to what so inspired him. He stayed with the band till the last member of it disappeared up a staircase in an office-building, down at the business end of the street; and even after that he lingered a while, looking at the staircase.

Finally, however, he set his face toward home, whither he marched in a procession, the visible part of which consisted of himself alone. All the way the rhythmic movements of his head kept time with his marching feet and, also, with a slight rise and fall of his fingers at about the median line of his abdomen. And pedestrians who encountered him in this preoccupation were not surprised to hear, as he passed, a few explosive little vocalizations: "Taw, p'taw-p'taw! TAW! Taw-aw-HAW!"

These were the outward symptoms of no fleeting impulse, but of steadfast desire; therefore they were persistent. The likeness of the great bass horn remained upon the retina of his mind's eye, losing nothing of its brazen enormity with the passing of hours, nor abating, in his mind's ear, one whit of its fascinating blatancy. Penrod might have forgotten almost anything else more readily; for such a horn has this double compulsion: people cannot possibly keep themselves from looking at its possessor—and they certainly have GOT to listen to him!

Penrod was preoccupied at dinner and during the evening, now and then causing his father some irritation by croaking, "Taw, p'taw-p'taw!" while the latter was talking. And when bedtime came for the son of the house, he mounted the stairs in a rhythmic manner, and p'tawed himself through the upper hall as far as his own chamber.

Even after he had gone to bed, there came a revival of these manifestations. His mother had put out his light for him and had returned to the library downstairs; three-quarters of an hour had elapsed since then, and Margaret was in her room, next to his, when a continuous low croaking (which she was just able to bear) suddenly broke out into loud, triumphal blattings:

"ᴛᴀᴡ, p'taw-p'taw-aw-HAW! P'taw-WAW-aw! Aw-PAW!"

"Penrod," Margaret called, "stop that! I'm trying to write letters. If you don't quit and go to sleep, I'll call papa up, and you'll *see !*"

The noise ceased, or, rather, it tapered down to a desultory faint croaking which finally died out; but there can be little doubt that Penrod's last waking thoughts were of instrumental music. And in the morning, when he woke to face the gloomy day's scholastic tasks, something unusual and eager dawned in his face with the return of memory. "Taw-p'taw!" he began. "ᴘᴀᴡ!"

All day, in school and out, his mind was busy with computations—not such as are prescribed by mathematical pedants, but estimates of how much old rags and old iron would sell for enough money to buy a horn. Happily, the next day, at lunch, he was able to dismiss this problem from his mind: he learned that his Uncle Joe would be passing through town, on his way from Nevada, the following after-noon, and all the Schofield family were to go to the station to see him. Penrod would be excused from school.

At this news his cheeks became pink, and for a moment he was breathless. Uncle Joe and Penrod did not meet often, but, when they did, Uncle Joe invariably gave Penrod money. Moreover, he always managed to do it privately, so that later there was no bothersome supervision. Last time he had given Penrod a silver dollar.

At thirty-five minutes after two, Wednesday afternoon, Uncle Joe's train came into the station, and Uncle Joe got out and shouted among his relatives. At eighteen minutes before three he was waving to them from the platform of the last car, having just slipped a two-dollar bill into Penrod's breast-pocket. And, at seven minutes after three, Penrod opened the door of the largest "music store" in town.

A tall, exquisite, fair man, evidently a musical earl, stood before him, leaning whimsically upon a piano of the highest polish. The sight abashed Penrod not a bit—his remarkable financial condition even made him rather peremptory.

"See here," he said brusquely: "I want to look at that big horn in the window."

"Very well," said the earl; "look at it." And he leaned more luxuriously upon the polished piano.

"I meant——" Penrod began, but paused, something daunted, while an unnamed fear brought greater mildness into his voice, as he continued, "I meant —I—— How much *is* that big horn?"

"How much?" the earl repeated.

"I mean," said Penrod, "how much is it worth?"

"I don't know," the earl returned. "Its price is eighty-five dollars."

"Eighty-fi——" Penrod began mechanically, but was forced to pause and swallow a little air that obstructed his throat, as the difference between eighty-five and two became more and more startling. He had entered the store, rich; in the last ten seconds he had become poverty-stricken. Eighty-five dollars was the same as eighty-five millions.

"Shall I put it aside for you," asked the salesman-earl, "while you look around the other stores to see if there's anything you like better?"

"I guess—I guess not," said Penrod, whose face had grown red. He swallowed again, scraped the floor with the side of his right shoe, scratched the back of his neck, and then, trying to make his manner casual and easy, "Well I can't stand around here all day," he said. "I got to be gettin' on up the street."

"Business, I suppose?"

Penrod, turning to the door, suspected jocularity, but he found himself without recourse; he was non-plussed.

"Sure you won't let me have that horn tied up in nice wrapping-paper in case you decide to take it?"

Penrod was almost positive that the spirit of this question was satirical; but he was unable to reply, except by a feeble shake of the head—though ten minutes later, as he plodded forlornly his homeward way, he looked over his shoulder and sent backward a few words of morose repartee:

"Oh, I am, am I?" he muttered, evidently concluding a conversation which he had continued mentally with the salesman. "Well, you're double anything you call me, so that makes you a smart Aleck twice! Ole double smart Aleck!"

After that, he walked with the least bit more briskness, but not much. No wonder he felt discouraged: there are times when eighty-five dollars can be a blow to anybody! Penrod was so stunned that he actually forgot what was in his pocket. He

passed two drug stores, and they had absolutely no
meaning to him. He walked all the way without
spending a cent.

At home he spent a moment in the kitchen pantry
while the cook was in the cellar; then he went out
to the stable and began some really pathetic experiments. His materials were the small tin funnel
which he had obtained in the pantry, and a short
section of old garden hose. He inserted the funnel
into one end of the garden hose, and made it fast
by wrappings of cord. Then he arranged the hose
in a double, circular coil, tied it so that it would
remain coiled, and blew into the other end.

He blew and blew and blew; he set his lips tight
together, as he had observed the little musician with
the big horn set his, and blew and sputtered, and
sputtered and blew, but nothing of the slightest importance happened in the orifice of the funnel. Still
he blew. He began to be dizzy; his eyes watered;
his expression became as horrible as a strangled
person's. He but blew the more. He stamped his
feet and blew. He staggered to the wheelbarrow,
sat, and blew—and yet the funnel uttered nothing;
it seemed merely to breathe hard.

It would not sound like a horn, and, when Penrod

'finally gave up, he had to admit piteously that it
did not look like a horn. No boy over nine could
have pretended that it was a horn.

He tossed the thing upon the floor, and leaned
back in the wheelbarrow, inert.

"Yay, Penrod!"

Sam Williams appeared in the doorway, and,
behind Sam, Master Roderick Magsworth Bitts,
Junior.

"Yay, there!"

Penrod made no response.

The two came in, and Sam picked up the poor
contrivance Penrod had tossed upon the floor.

"What's this ole dingus?" Sam asked.

"Nothin'."

"Well, what's it for?"

"Nothin'," said Penrod. "It's a kind of a horn."

"What kind?"

"For music," said Penrod simply.

Master Bitts laughed loud and long; he was de-
risive. "Music!" he yipped. "I thought you
meant a cow's horn! He says it's a music-horn,
Sam? What you think o' that?"

Sam blew into the thing industriously.

"It won't work," he announced.

"Course it won't!" Roddy Bitts shouted. "You can't make it go without you got a *real* horn. I'm goin' to get me a real horn some day before long, and then you'll see me goin' up and down here playin' it like sixty! I'll——"

"'Some day before long!'" Sam mocked. "Yes, we will! Why'n't you get it to-day, if you're goin' to?"

"I would," said Roddy. "I'd go get the money from my father right now, only he wouldn't give it to me.".

Sam whooped, and Penrod, in spite of his great depression, uttered a few jibing sounds.

"I'd get *my* father to buy me a fire-engine and team o' *horses*," Sam bellowed, "only he wouldn't!"

"Listen, can't you?" cried Roddy. "I mean he would most any time, but not this month. I can't have any money for a month beginning last Saturday, because I got paint on one of our dogs, and he came in the house with it on him, and got some on pretty near everything. If it hadn't 'a' been for that——"

"Oh, yes!" said Sam. "If it hadn't 'a' been for that! It's always *sumpthing !*"

"It is not!"

"Well, then, why'n't you go *get* a real horn?"

Roddy's face had flushed with irritation.

"Well, didn't I just *tell* you——" he began, but paused, while the renewal of some interesting recollection became visible in his expression. "Why, I could, if I wanted to," he said more calmly. "It wouldn't be a new one, maybe. I guess it would be kind of an old one, but——"

"Oh, a toy horn!" said Sam. "I expect one you had when you were three years old, and your mother tuck it up in the attic to keep till you're dead, or sumpthing!"

"It's not either any toy horn," Roddy insisted. 'It's a reg'lar horn for a band, and I could have it is easy as anything."

The tone of this declaration was so sincere that it roused the lethargic Penrod.

"Roddy, is that true?" he sat up to inquire piercingly.

"Of course it is!" Master Bitts returned. "What you take me for? I could go get that horn this minute if I wanted to."

"A real one—honest?"

"Well, didn't I say it was a real one?"

"Like in the *band*?"

"I said so, didn't I?"

"I guess you mean one of those little ones," said Penrod.

"No, sir!" Roddy insisted stoutly; "it's a big one! It winds around in a big circle that would go all the way around a pretty fat man."

"What store is it in?"

"It's not in any store," said Roddy. "It's at my Uncle Ethelbert's. He's got this horn and three or four pianos and a couple o' harps and——"

"Does he keep a music store?"

"No. These harps and pianos and all such are old ones—awful old."

"Oh," said Sam, "he runs a second-hand store!"

"He does not!" Master Bitts returned angrily "He doesn't do anything. He's just *got* 'em. He's got forty-one guitars——"

"Yay!" Sam whooped, and jumped up and down "Listen to Roddy Bitts makin' up lies!"

"You look out, Sam Williams!" said Roddy threateningly. "You look out how you call me names!"

"What name'd I call you?"

"You just the same as said I told lies. That's just as good as callin' me a liar, isn't it?"

"No," said Sam; "but I got a right to, if I want
ɔ. Haven't I, Penrod?"

"How?" Roddy demanded hotly. "How you
ot a right to?"

"Because you can't prove what you said."

"Well," said Roddy, "you'd be just as much of
ne if you can't prove what I said *wasn't* true."

"No, sir! You either got to prove it or be a liar.
sn't that so, Penrod.

"Yes, sir," Penrod ruled, with a little importance.
That's the way it is, Roddy."

"Well, then," said Roddy, "come on over to my
ncle Ethelbert's, and I'll show you!"

"No," said Sam. "I wouldn't walk over there
ıst to find out sumpthing I already know isn't so.
ıutside of a music store there isn't anybody in the
orld got forty-one guitars! I've heard lots o'
eople *talk*, but I never heard such a big l——"

"You shut up!" shouted Roddy. "You ole——"
Penrod interposed.

"Why'n't you show us the horn, Roddy?" he asked.
You said you could get it. You show us the horn
nd we'll believe you. If you show us the horn,
am'll haf to take what he said back; won't you,
am?"

"Yes," said Sam, and added: "He hasn't go
any. He went and told a——"

Roddy's eyes were bright with rage; he breathe
noisily.

"I haven't?" he cried. "You just wait here, an
I'll show you!"

And he ran furiously from the stable.

CHAPTER XXII

THE HORN OF FAME

B ET he won't come back!" said Sam.

"Well, he might."

"Well, if he does and he hasn't got any horn, I got a right to call him anything I want to, nd he's got to stand it. And if he doesn't come ack," Sam continued, as by the code, "then I got right to call him whatever I like next time I ketch m out."

"I expect he'll have *some* kind of ole horn, maybe," id Penrod.

"No," the skeptical Sam insisted, "he won't."

But Roddy did. Twenty minutes elapsed, and oth the waiting boys had decided that they were gally entitled to call him whatever they thought ting, when he burst in, puffing; and in his hands he re a horn. It was a "real" one, and of a kind at neither Penrod nor Sam had ever seen before, ough they failed to realize this, because its shape as instantly familiar to them. No horn could have

been simpler: it consisted merely of one circular coil
of brass with a mouthpiece at one end for the musician, and a wide-flaring mouth of its own, for the
noise, at the other.   But it was obviously a second-
hand horn; dents slightly marred it, here and there,
and its surface was dull, rather greenish.   There
were no keys; and a badly faded green cord and
tassel hung from the coil.

Even so shabby a horn as this electrified Penrod.
It was not a stupendous horn, but it was a horn;
and when a boy has been sighing for the moon, a
piece of green cheese will satisfy him, for he can
play that it is the moon.

"Gimme that *horn!*" Penrod shouted, as he dashed
for it.

"*Yay!*" Sam cried, and sought to wrest it from
him.   Roddy joined the scuffle, trying to retain
the horn; but Penrod managed to secure it.   With
one free hand he fended the others off while he blew
into the mouthpiece.

"Let me have it," Sam urged.   "You can't do
anything with it.   Lemme take it, Penrod."

"No!" said Roddy.   "Let *me!*   My goodness!
Ain't I got any right to blow my own horn?"

They pressed upon Penrod, who frantically fended

nd frantically blew. At last he remembered to
ompress his lips, and force the air through the com-
ression.

A magnificent snort from the horn was his reward.
Ie removed his lips from the mouthpiece, and capered
ı pride.

"Hah!" he cried. "Hear that? I guess *I* can't
lay this good ole horn! Oh, no!"

During his capers, Sam captured the horn. But
am had not made the best of his opportunities
s an observer of bands; he thrust the mouthpiece
eep into his mouth, and blew until his expression
ecame one of agony.

"No, no!" Penrod exclaimed. "You haven't got
ıe secret of blowin' a horn, Sam. What's the use
our keepin' hold of it, when you don't know any
ıore about it 'n that? It ain't makin' a sound!
ou lemme have that good ole horn back, Sam.
Iaven't you got sense enough to see I know how
ı *play ?*"

Laying hands upon it, he jerked it away from Sam,
ho was a little piqued over the failure of his own
forts, especially as Penrod now produced a son-
ıous blat—quite a long one. Sam became cross.

"My goodness!" Roddy Bitts said peevishly.

"Ain't I ever goin' to get a turn at my own horn? Here you've had two turns, Penrod, and even Sam Williams——"

Sam's petulance at once directed itself toward Roddy partly because of the latter's tactless use of the word "even," and the two engaged in controversy, while Penrod was left free to continue the experiments which so enraptured him.

"Your own horn!" Sam sneered. "I bet it isn't yours! Anyway, you can't prove it's yours, and that gives me a right to call you any——"

"You better not! It is, too, mine. It's just the same as mine!"

"No, sir," said Sam; "I bet you got to take it back where you got it, and that's not anything like the same as yours; so I got a perfect right to call you whatev——"

"I do *not* haf to take it back where I got it, either!" Roddy cried, more and more irritated by his opponent's persistence in stating his rights in this matter.

"I *bet* they told you to bring it back," said Sam tauntingly.

"They didn't, either! There wasn't anybody there."

"Yay! Then you got to get it back before they know it's gone."

"I don't either any such a thing! I heard my Uncle Ethelbert say Sunday he didn't want it. He said he wished somebody'd take that horn off his hands so's he could buy sumpthing else. That's just exactly what he said. I heard him tell my mother. He said, 'I guess I prackly got to give it away if I'm ever goin' to get rid of it.' Well, when my own uncle says he wants to give a horn away, and he wishes he could get rid of it, I guess it's just the same as mine, soon as I go and take it, isn't it? I'm goin' to keep it."

Sam was shaken, but he had set out to demonstrate those rights of his and did not mean to yield them.

"Yes; you'll have a *nice* time," he said, "next time your uncle goes to play on that horn and can't find it. No, sir; I got a perfect ri——"

"My uncle don't *play* on it!" Roddy shrieked. "It's an ole wore-out horn nobody wants, and it's mine, I tell you! I can blow on it, or bust it, or kick it out in the alley and leave it there, if I want to!"

"No, you can't!"

"I can, too!"

"No, you can't. You can't *prove* you can, and unless you prove it, I got a perf——"

Roddy stamped his foot. "I can, too!" he shrieked. "You ole durn jackass, I can, too! I can, can, can, can——"

. Penrod suddenly stopped his intermittent production of blats, and intervened. "*I* know how you can prove it, Roddy," he said briskly. "There's one way anybody can always prove sumpthing belongs to them, so that nobody'd have a right to call them what they wanted to. You can prove it's yours, *easy !*"

"How?"

"Well," said Penrod, "if you give it away."

"What you mean?" asked Roddy, frowning.

"Well, look here," Penrod began brightly. "You can't give anything away that doesn't belong to you, can you?"

"No."

"So, then," the, resourceful boy continued, "f'r instance, if you give this ole horn to me, that'd prove it was yours, and Sam'd haf to say it was, and he wouldn't have any right to——"

"I won't do it!" said Roddy sourly. "I don't

want to give you that horn. What I want to give
you anything at all for?"

Penrod sighed, as if the task of reaching Roddy's
mind with reason were too heavy for him. "Well, if
you don't want to prove it, and rather let us have
the right to call you anything we want to—well, all
right, then," he said.

"You look out what you call me!" Roddy cried,
only the more incensed, in spite of the pains Penrod
was taking with him. "I don't haf to prove it.
It's *mine !*"

"What kind o' proof is that?" Sam Williams demanded severely. "You *got* to prove it and you
can't do it!"

Roddy began a reply, but his agitation was so
great that what he said had not attained coherency
when Penrod again intervened. He had just remembered something important.

"Oh, *I* know, Roddy!" he exclaimed. "If you
sell it, that'd prove it was yours almost as good as
givin' it away. What'll you take for it?"

"I don't want to sell it," said Roddy sulkily.

"Yay! Yay! YAY!" shouted the taunting Sam
Williams, whose every word and sound had now
become almost unbearable to Master Bitts. Sam

was usually so good-natured that the only explanation of his conduct must lie in the fact that Roddy constitutionally got on his nerves. "He *knows* he can't prove it! He's a goner, and now we can begin callin' him anything we can think of! I choose to call him one first, Penrod. Roddy, you're a——"

"Wait!" shouted Penrod, for he really believed Roddy's claims to be both moral and legal. When an uncle who does not even play upon an old second-hand horn wishes to get rid of that horn, and even complains of having it on his hands, it seems reasonable to consider that the horn becomes the property of a nephew who has gone to the trouble of carrying the undesired thing out of the house.

Penrod determined to deal fairly. The difference between this horn and the one in the "music-store" window seemed to him just about the difference between two and eighty-five. He drew forth the green bill from his pocket.

"Roddy," he said, "I'll give you two dollars for that horn."

Sam Williams's mouth fell open; he was silenced indeed. But for a moment, the confused and badgered Roddy was incredulous; he had not dreamed that Penrod possessed such a sum.

"Lemme take a look at that money!" he said.

If at first there had been in Roddy's mind a little doubt about his present rights of ownership, he had talked himself out of it. Also, his financial supplies for the month were cut off, on account of the careless dog. Finally, he thought that the horn was worth about fifty cents.

"I'll do it, Penrod!" he said with decision.

Thereupon Penrod shouted aloud, prancing up and down the carriage-house with the horn. Roddy was happy, too, and mingled his voice with Penrod's.

"Hi! Hi! Hi!" shouted Roddy Bitts. "I'm goin' to buy me an air-gun down at Fox's hardware store!"

And he departed, galloping.

. . . He returned the following afternoon. School was over, and Penrod and Sam were again in the stable; Penrod "was practising" upon the horn, with Sam for an unenthusiastic spectator and auditor. Master Bitts' brow was heavy; he looked uneasy.

"Penrod," he began, "I got to——"

Penrod removed the horn briefly from his lips.

"Don't come bangin' around here and interrup' me all the time," he said severely. "I got to practise."

And he again pressed the mouthpiece to his lips. He was not of those whom importance makes gracious.

"Look here, Penrod," said Roddy, "I got to have that horn back."

Penrod lowered the horn quickly enough at this.

"What you talkin' about?" he demanded. "What you want to come bangin' around here for and——"

"I came around here for that horn," Master Bitts returned, and his manner was both dogged and apprehensive, the apprehension being more prevalent when he looked at Sam. "I got to have that horn," he said.

Sam, who had been sitting in the wheelbarrow, jumped up and began to dance triumphantly.

"Yay! It *wasn't* his, after all! Roddy Bitts told a big l——"

"I never, either!" Roddy almost wailed.

"Well, what you want the horn back for?" the terrible Sam demanded.

"Well, 'cause I want it. I got a right to want it if I want to, haven't I?"

Penrod's face had flushed with indignation.

"You look here, Sam," he began hotly. "Didn't you hear Roddy say this was his horn?"

"He said it!" Sam declared. "He said it a million times!"

"Well, and didn't he sell this horn to me?"

"Yes, *sir !*"

"Didn't I pay him money cash down for it?"

"Two dollars!"

"Well, and ain't it my horn now, Sam?"

"You bet you!"

"*Yes*, sir!" Penrod went on with vigour. "It's my horn now whether it belonged to you or not, Roddy, because you *sold* it to me and I paid my good ole money for it. I guess a thing belongs to the person that paid their own money for it, doesn't it? *I* don't haf to give up my own propaty, even if you did come on over here and told us a big l——"

"I *never !*" shouted Roddy. "It was my horn, too, and I didn't tell any such a thing!" He paused; then, reverting to his former manner, said stubbornly, "I got to have that horn back. I *got* to!"

"Why'n't you tell us what *for*, then?" Sam insisted.

Roddy's glance at this persecutor was one of anguish.

"I know my own biz'nuss!" he muttered.

And while Sam jeered, Roddy turned to Penrod desperately.

"You gimme that horn back! I got to have it."
But Penrod followed Sam's lead.

"Well, why can't you tell us what *for?*" he asked.

Perhaps if Sam had not been there, Roddy could have unbosomed himself. He had no doubt of his own virtue in this affair, and he was conscious that he had acted in good faith throughout—though, perhaps, a little impulsively. But he was in a predicament, and he knew that if he became more explicit, Sam could establish with undeniable logic those rights about which he had been so odious the day before. Such triumph for Sam was not within Roddy's power to contemplate; he felt that he would rather die, or sumpthing.

"I got to have that horn!" he reiterated woodenly.

Penrod had no intention to humour this preposterous boy, and it was only out of curiosity that he asked, "Well, if you want the horn back, where's the two dollars?"

"I spent it. I bought an air-gun for a dollar and sixty-five cents, and three sodies and some candy with the rest. I'll owe you the two dollars, Penrod. I'm willing to do that much."

"Well, why don't you give him the air-gun," asked the satirical Sam, "and owe him the rest?"

"I can't. Papa took the air-gun away from me because he didn't like sumpthing I did with it. I got to owe you the whole two dollars, Penrod."

"Look here, Roddy," said Penrod. "Don't you s'pose I'd rather keep this horn and blow on it than have you owe me two dollars?"

There was something about this simple question which convinced Roddy that his cause was lost. His hopes had been but faint from the beginning of the interview.

"Well——" said Roddy. For a time he scuffed the floor with his shoe. "Daw-gone it!" he said, at last; and he departed morosely.

Penrod had already begun to "practise" again, and Mr. Williams, after vain appeals to be permitted to practise in turn, sank into the wheelbarrow in a state of boredom, not remarkable under the circumstances. Then Penrod contrived—it may have been accidental—to produce at one blast two tones which varied in pitch.

His pride and excitement were extreme though not contagious. "Listen, Sam!" he shouted. "How's *that* for high?"

The bored Sam made no response other than to rise languidly to his feet, stretch, and start for home.

Left alone, Penrod's practice became less ardent;
he needed the stimulus of an auditor. With the
horn upon his lap he began to rub the greenish brass
surface with a rag. He meant to make this good ole
two-dollar horn of his *look* like sumpthing!

Presently, moved by a better idea, he left the horn
in the stable and went into the house, soon afterward
appearing before his mother in the library.

"Mamma," he said, complainingly, "Della
won't——"

But Mrs. Schofield checked him.

"Sh, Penrod; your father's reading the paper."

Penrod glanced at Mr. Schofield, who sat near the
window, reading by the last light of the early sunset.

"Well, I know it," said Penrod, lowering his voice.
"But I wish you'd tell Della to let me have the
silver polish. She says she won't, and I want to——"

"Be quiet, Penrod, you can't have the silver
polish."

"But, mamma——"

"Not another word. Can't you see you're inter-
rupting your father. Go on, papa."

Mr. Schofield read aloud several despatches from
abroad, and after each one of them Penrod began in
a low but pleading tone:

"Mamma, I want——"

"*Sh*, Penrod!"

Mr. Schofield continued to read, and Penrod remained in the room, for he was determined to have the silver polish.

"Here's something curious," said Mr. Schofield, as his eye fell upon a paragraph among the "locals."

"What?"

"Valuable relic missing," Mr. Schofield read. "It was reported at police headquarters to-day that a valuable object had been stolen from the collection of antique musical instruments owned by E. Magsworth Bitts, 724 Central Avenue. The police insist that it must have been an inside job, but Mr. Magsworth Bitts inclines to think it was the work of a negro, as only one article was removed and nothing else found to be disturbed. The object stolen was an ancient hunting-horn dating from the eighteenth century and claimed to have belonged to Louis XV, King of France. It was valued at about twelve hundred and fifty dollars."

Mrs. Schofield opened her mouth wide. "Why, that *is* curious!" she exclaimed.

She jumped up. "Penrod!"

But Penrod was no longer in the room.

"What's the matter?" Mr. Schofield inquired.

"Penrod!" said Mrs. Schofield breathlessly. "*He* bought an old horn—like one in old hunting-pictures—yesterday! He bought it with some money Uncle Joe gave him! He bought it from Roddy Bitts!"

"Where'd he go?"

Together they rushed to the back porch.

Penrod had removed the lid of the cistern; he was kneeling beside it, and the fact that the diameter of the opening into the cistern was one inch less than the diameter of the coil of Louis the Fifteenth's hunting-horn was all that had just saved Louis the Fifteenth's hunting-horn from joining the drowned trousers of Herman.

Such was Penrod's instinct, and thus loyally he had followed it.

. . . He was dragged into the library, expecting anything whatever. The dreadful phrases of the newspaper item rang through his head like the gongs of delirium: "Police headquarters!" "Work of a negro!" "King of France!" "Valued at about twelve hundred and fifty dollars!"

Eighty-five dollars had dismayed him; twelve hundred and fifty was unthinkable. Nightmares were coming to life before his eyes.

But a light broke slowly; it came first to Mr. and Mrs. Schofield, and it was they who illuminated Penrod. Slowly, slowly, as they spoke more and more pleasantly to him, it began to dawn upon him that this trouble was all Roddy's.

And when Mr. Schofield went to take the horn to the house of Mr. Ethelbert Magsworth Bitts, Penrod sat quietly with his mother. Mr. Schofield was gone an hour and a half. Upon his solemn return he reported that Roddy's father had been summoned by telephone to bring his son to the house of Uncle Ethelbert. Mr. Bitts had forthwith appeared with Roddy, and, when Mr. Schofield came away, Roddy was still (after half an hour's previous efforts) explaining his honourable intentions. Mr. Schofield indicated that Roddy's condition was agitated, and that he was having a great deal of difficulty in making his position clear.

Penrod's imagination paused outside the threshold of that room in Mr. Ethelbert Magsworth Bitts' house, and awe fell upon him when he thought of it. Roddy seemed to have disappeared within

a shrouding mist where Penrod's mind refused to
follow him.

"Well, he got back his ole horn!" said Sam after
school the next afternoon. "I *knew* we had a perfect right to call him whatever we wanted to! I
bet you hated to give up that good ole horn, Penrod."

But Penrod was serene. He was even a little
superior.

"Pshaw!" he said. "I'm goin' to learn to play
on sumpthing better'n any ole horn. It's lots better,
because you can carry it around with you anywhere,
and you couldn't a horn."

"What is it?" Sam asked, not too much pleased
by Penrod's air of superiority and high content.
"You mean a jew's-harp?"

"I guess not! I mean a flute with all silver on it
and everything. My father's goin' to buy me one."

"I bet he isn't!"

"He is, too," said Penrod; "soon as I'm twenty-
one years old."

CHAPTER XXIII

THE PARTY

> *Miss Amy Rennsdale*
>
> *At Home*
> *Saturday, the twenty-third*
> *from three to six*
>
> *R. s. v. p.*   *Dancing*

THIS little card, delicately engraved, betokened the hospitality incidental to the ninth birthday anniversary of Baby Rennsdale, youngest member of the Friday Afternoon Dancing Class, and, by the same token, it represented the total social activity (during that season) of a certain limited bachelor set consisting of Messrs. Penrod Schofield and Samuel Williams. The truth must be faced: Penrod and Sam were seldom invited to small parties; they were considered too imaginative. But in the case of so large an affair as Miss Rennsdale's, the feeling that their parents would be sensitive outweighed fears of what Penrod and Sam might do at the party. Reputation is indeed a bubble, but sometimes it is blown of sticky stuff.

The comrades set out for the fête in company, final maternal outpourings upon deportment -and the duty of dancing with the hostess evaporating in their freshly cleaned ears. Both boys, however, were in a state of mind, body, and decoration appropriate to the gala scene they were approaching. Their collars were wide and white; inside the pockets of their overcoats were glistening dancing-pumps, wrapped in tissue-paper; inside their jacket pockets were pleasant-smelling new white gloves, and inside their heads solemn timidity commingled with glittering anticipations. Before them, like a Christmas tree glimpsed through lace curtains, they beheld joy shimmering—music, ice-cream, macaroons, tinsel caps, and the starched ladies of their hearts. Penrod and Sam walked demurely yet almost boundingly; their faces were shining but grave—they were on their way to the Party!

"Look at there!" said Penrod. "There's Carlie Chitten!"

"Where?" Sam asked.

"'Cross the street. Haven't you got any eyes?"

"Well, whyn't you say he was 'cross the street in the first place?" Sam returned plaintively. "Besides, he's so little you can't hardly see him." This was, of course, a violent exaggeration, though Master Chitten, not yet eleven years old, was an inch or two short for his age. "He's all dressed up," Sam added. "I guess he must be invited."

"I bet he does sumpthing," said Penrod.

"I bet he does, too," Sam agreed.

This was the extent of their comment upon the small person across the street, but, in spite of its non-committal character, the manner of both commentators seemed to indicate that they had just exchanged views upon an interesting and even curious subject. They walked along in silence for several minutes, staring speculatively at Master Chitten.

His appearance was pleasant and not remarkable. He was a handsome, dark little boy, with quick eyes and a precociously reserved expression; his air was "well-bred"; he was exquisitely neat, and he had a look of manly competence which grown people found attractive and reassuring. In short, he was a boy of whom a timid adult stranger would have inquired the way with confidence. And yet Sam and Penrod

had mysterious thoughts about him—obviously there
was something subterranean here.

They continued to look at him for the greater
part of a block, when, their progress bringing them
in sight of Miss Amy Rennsdale's place of residence,
their attention was directed to a group of men bearing festal burdens—encased violins, a shrouded harp,
and other beckoning shapes. There were signs, too,
that most of "those invited" intended to miss no
moment of this party; guests already indoors
watched from the windows the approach of the
musicians. Washed boys in black and white, and
girls in tender colours converged from various directions, making gayly for the thrilling gateway—and
the most beautiful little girl in all the world, Marjorie
Jones, of the amber curls, jumped from a carriage
step to the curbstone as Penrod and Sam came up.
She waved to them.

Sam responded heartily, but Penrod, feeling real
emotion and seeking to conceal it, muttered, "'Lo,
Marjorie!" gruffly, offering no further demonstration. Marjorie paused a moment, expectant, and
then, as he did not seize the opportunity to ask her
for the first dance, she tried not to look disappointed
and ran into the house ahead of the two boys. Pen-

rod was scarlet; he wished to dance the first dance
with Marjorie, and the second and the third and
all the other dances, and he strongly desired to sit
with her "at refreshments," but he had been unable
to ask for a single one of these privileges. It would
have been impossible for him to state why he was
thus dumb, although the reason was simple and
wholly complimentary to Marjorie: she had looked
so overpoweringly pretty that she had produced in
the bosom of her admirer a severe case of stage fright.
That was "all the matter with him," but it was the
beginning of his troubles, and he did not recover
until he and Sam reached the "gentleman's dressing-
room," whither they were directed by a polite
coloured man.

Here they found a cloud of acquaintances getting
into pumps and gloves, and, in a few extreme cases,
readjusting hair before a mirror. Some even went
so far—after removing their shoes and putting on
their pumps—as to wash traces of blacking from their
hands in the adjacent bathroom before assuming their
gloves. Penrod, being in a strange mood, was one
of these, sharing the basin with little Maurice Levy.

"Carlie Chitten's here," said Maurice, as they
soaped their hands.

"I guess I know it," Penrod returned. "I bet he does sumpthing, too."

Maurice shook his head ominously. "Well, I'm gettin' tired of it. I know he was the one stuck that cold fried egg in P'fesser Bartet's overcoat pocket at dancin'-school, and ole p'fesser went and blamed it on me. Then, Carlie, he c'm up to me, th' other day, and he says, 'Smell my buttonhole bokay.' He had some vi'lets stickin' in his buttonhole, and I went to smell 'em and water squirted on me out of 'em. I guess I've stood about enough, and if he does another thing I don't like, he better look out!"

Penrod showed some interest, inquiring for details, whereupon Maurice explained that if Master Chitten displeased him further, Master Chitten would receive a blow upon one of his features. Maurice was simple and homely about it, seeking rhetorical vigour rather than elegance; in fact, what he definitely promised Master Chitten was "a bang on the snoot."

"Well," said Penrod, "he never bothered *me* any. I expect he knows too much for that!"

A cry of pain was heard from the dressing-room at this juncture, and, glancing through the doorway,

Maurice and Penrod beheld Sam Williams in the act
of sucking his right thumb with vehemence, the
while his brow was contorted and his eyes watered.
He came into the bathroom and held his thumb under
a faucet.

"That darn little Carlie Chitten!" he complained,
"He ast me to hold a little tin box he showed me. He
told me to hold it between my thumb and fingers and
he'd show me sumpthing. Then he pushed the lid,
and a big needle came out of a hole and stuck me half
through my thumb. That's a *nice* way to act, isn't
it?"

Carlie Chitten's dark head showed itself cautiously beyond the casing of the door.

"How's your thumb, Sam?" he asked.

"You wait!" Sam shouted, turning furiously, but
the small prestidigitator was gone. With a smothered laugh, Carlie dashed through the groups of boys
in the dressing-room and made his way downstairs,
his manner reverting to its usual polite gravity before
he entered the drawing-room, where his hostess
waited. Music sounding at about this time, he was
followed by the other boys, who came trooping down,
leaving the dressing-room empty.

Penrod, among the tail-enders of the procession,

made his dancing-school bow to Miss Rennsdale and
her grown-up supporters (two maiden aunts and a
governess) then he looked about for Marjorie, discovering her but too easily. Her amber curls were
swaying gently in time to the music; she looked
never more beautiful, and her partner was Master
Chitten!

A pang of great penetrative power and equal un-
expectedness found the most vulnerable spot beneath the simple black of Penrod Schofield's jacket.
Straightway he turned his back upon the crash-
covered floors where the dancers were, and moved
gloomily toward the hall. But one of the maiden
aunts Rennsdale waylaid him.

"It's Penrod Schofield, isn't it?" she asked. "Or
Sammy Williams? I'm not sure which. Is it Penrod?"

"Ma'am?" he said. "Yes'm."

"Well, Penrod, I can find a partner for you. There
are several dear little girls over here, if you'll come
with me."

"Well——" He paused, shifted from one foot to
the other, and looked enigmatic. "I better not," he
said. He meant no offence; his trouble was only
that he had not yet learned how to do as he pleased

at a party and, at the same time, to seem polite about it. "I guess I don't want to," he added.

"Very well!" And Miss Rennsdale instantly left him to his own devices.

He went to lurk in the wide doorway between the hall and the drawing-room—under such conditions the universal refuge of his sex at all ages. There he found several boys of notorious shyness, and stood with them in a mutually protective group. Now and then one of them would lean upon another until repelled by action and a husky "What's matter 'th you? Get off o' me!" They all twisted their slender necks uneasily against the inner bands of their collars at intervals, and sometimes exchanged facetious blows under cover. In the distance Penrod caught glimpses of amber curls flashing to and fro, and he knew himself to be among the derelicts.

He remained in this questionable sanctuary during the next dance, but, edging along the wall to lean more comfortably in a corner, as the music of the third sounded, he overheard part of a conversation which somewhat concerned him. The participants were the governess of his hostess, Miss Lowe, and that one of the aunts Rennsdale who had offered to provide him with a partner. These two ladies were stand-

ing just in front of him, unconscious of his near-
ness.

"I never," said Miss Rennsdale, "*never* saw a more
fascinating little boy than that Carlie Chitten.
There'll be some heartaches when he grows up; I
can't keep my eyes off him."

"Yes; he's a charming boy," said Miss Lowe.
"His manners are remarkable."

"He's a little man of the world," the enthusiastic
Miss Rennsdale went on, "very different from such
boys as Penrod Schofield!"

"Oh, *Penrod!*" Miss Lowe exclaimed. "Good
gracious!"

"I don't see why he came. He declines to dance—
rudely, too!"

"I don't think the little girls will mind *that* so
much!" Miss Lowe said. "If you'd come to the dancing class some Friday with Amy and me, you'd understand why."

They moved away. Penrod heard his name again
mentioned between them as they went, and though
he did not catch the accompanying remark, he was
inclined to think it unfavourable. He remained
where he was, brooding morbidly.

He understood that the government was against

him, nor was his judgment at fault in this conclusion. He was affected, also, by the conduct of Marjorie, who was now dancing gayly with Maurice Levy, a former rival of Penrod's. The fact that Penrod had not gone near her did not make her culpability seem the less; in his gloomy heart he resolved not to ask her for one single dance. He would not go near her. He would not go near *any of 'em!*

His eyes began to burn, and he swallowed heavily; but he was never one to succumb piteously to such emotion, and it did not even enter his head that he was at liberty to return to his own home. Neither he nor any of his friends had ever left a party until it was officially concluded. What his sufferings demanded of him now for their alleviation was not departure but action!

Underneath the surface, nearly all children's parties contain a group of outlaws who wait only for a leader to hoist the black flag. The group consists mainly of boys too shy to be at ease with the girls, but who wish to distinguish themselves in some way; and there are others, ordinarily well behaved, whom the mere actuality of a party makes drunken. The effect of music, too, upon children is incalculable, especially when they do not hear it often—and both a snare-drum and a bass drum were in the expensive orchestra at the Rennsdale party.

·Nevertheless, the outlawry at any party may remain incipient unless a chieftain appears, but in Penrod's corner were now gathering into one anarchical·mood all the necessary qualifications for leadership. Out of that bitter corner there stepped, not a Penrod Schofield subdued and hoping to win the lost favour of the Authorities, but a hot-hearted rebel determined on an uprising.

Smiling a reckless and challenging smile, he returned to the cluster of boys in the wide doorway and began to push one and another of them about. They responded hopefully with counter-pushes, and presently there was a tumultuous surging and eddying in that quarter, accompanied by noises which began to compete with the music. Then Penrod allowed himself to be shoved out among the circling dancers, so that he collided with Marjorie and Maurice Levy, almost oversetting them.

He made a mock bow and a mock apology, being inspired to invent a jargon phrase.

"Excuse me," he said, at the same time making vocal his own conception of a taunting laugh. "Excuse me, but I must 'a' got your bumpus!"

"He made a mock bow and a mock apology, being inspired to invent a jargon phrase. 'Excuse me,' he said, at the same time making vocal his own conception of a taunting laugh; 'excuse me, but I must 'a' got your bumpus!'"

Marjorie looked grieved and turned away with Maurice, but the boys in the doorway squealed with maniac laughter.

"Gotcher bumpus! Gotcher bumpus!" they shrilled. And they began to push others of their number against the dancing couples, shouting, "'Scuse me! Gotcher bumpus!"

It became a contagion and then a game. As the dances went on, strings of boys, led by Penrod, pursued one another across the rooms, howling, "Gotcher bumpus!" at the top of their lungs. They dodged and ducked, and seized upon dancers as shields; they caromed from one couple into another, and even into the musicians of the orchestra. Boys who were dancing abandoned their partners and joined the marauders, shrieking, "Gotcher bumpus!" Potted plants went down; a slender gilt chair refused to support the hurled body of Master Roderick Magsworth Bitts, and the sound of splintering wood mingled with other sounds. Dancing became impossible; Miss Amy Rennsdale wept in the midst of the riot, and everybody knew that Penrod Schofield had "started it."

Under instructions, the leader of the orchestra, clapping his hands for attention, stepped to the centre of the drawing-room, and shouted,

"A moment silence, if you bleace!"

Slowly the hubbub ceased; the virtuous and the wicked paused alike in their courses to listen. Miss Amy Rennsdale was borne away to have her tearful face washed, and Marjorie Jones and Carlie Chitten and Georgie Bassett came forward consciously, escorted by Miss Lowe. The musician waited until the return of the small hostess; then he announced in a loud voice:

"A fency dence called 'Les Papillons', denced by Miss Amy Rennstul, Miss Chones, Mister Chorch Passett, ant Mister Jitten. Some young chentlemen haf mate so much noise ant confoosion, Miss Lowe wish me to ask bleace no more such a nonsense. Fency dence, 'Les Papillons.' "

Thereupon, after formal salutations, Mr. Chitten took Marjorie's hand, Georgie Bassett took Miss Rennsdale's, and they proceeded to dance "Les Papillons" in a manner which made up in conscientiousness whatever it may have lacked in abandon. The outlaw leader looked on, smiling a smile intended to represent careless contempt, but in reality he was unpleasantly surprised. A fancy dance by Georgie Bassett and Baby Rennsdale was customary at every party attended by members of the Friday Afternoon

Dancing Class, but Marjorie and Carlie Chitten were new performers, and Penrod had not heard that they had learned to dance "Les Papillons" together. He was the further embittered.

Carlie made a false step, recovering himself with some difficulty, whereupon a loud, jeering squawk of laughter was heard from the insurgent cluster, which had been awed to temporary quiet but still maintained its base in the drawing-room doorway. There was a general "*Sh!*" followed by a shocked whispering, as well as a general turning of eyes toward Penrod. But it was not Penrod who had laughed, though no one would have credited him with an alibi. The laughter came from two throats that breathed as one with such perfect simultaneousness that only one was credited with the disturbance. These two throats belonged respectively to Samuel Williams and Maurice Levy, who were standing in a strikingly Rosencrantz-and-Guildenstern attitude.

"He got me with his ole tin-box needle, too," Maurice muttered to Sam. "He was goin' to do it to Marjorie, and I told her to look out, and he says, 'Here, *you* take it!' all of a sudden, and he stuck it in my hand so quick I never thought. And then, *bim!*

his ole needle shot out and perty near went through
my thumb-bone or sumpthing. He'll be sorry before
this day's over!"

"Well," said Sam darkly, "he's goin' to be sorry
he stuck *me*, anyway!" Neither Sam nor Maurice
had even the vaguest plan for causing the desired
regret in the breast of Master Chitten, but both
derived a little consolation from these prophecies.
And they, too, had aligned themselves with the insur-
gents. , Their motives were personal—Carlie Chitten
had wronged both of them, and Carlie was conspicuously in high favour with the Authorities. Naturally
Sam and Maurice were against the Authorities.

"Les Papillons" came to a conclusion. Carlie and
Georgie bowed; Marjorie Jones and Baby Rennsdale courtesied, and there was loud applause. In
fact, the demonstration became so uproarious that
some measure of it was open to suspicion, especially
as hisses of reptilian venomousness were commingled
with it, and also a hoarse but vociferous repetition
of the dastard words, "Carlie dances *rotten!*" Again
it was the work of Rosencrantz and Guildenstern,
but the plot was attributed to another.

"*Shame*, Penrod Schofield!" said both the aunts
Rennsdale publicly, and Penrod, wholly innocent,

became scarlet with indignant mortification. Carlie
Chitten himself, however, marked the true offenders.
A slight flush tinted his cheeks, and then, in his quiet,
self-contained way, he slipped through the crowd of
girls and boys, unnoticed, into the hall, and ran noiselessly up the stairs and into the "gentlemen's dressing room," now inhabited only by hats, caps, overcoats, and the temporarily discarded shoes of the
dancers. Most of the shoes stood in rows against
the wall, and Carlie examined these rows attentively,
after a time discovering a pair of shoes with patent
leather tips.   He knew them; they belonged to Maurice Levy, and picking them up, he went to a corner
of the room where four shoes had been left together
under a chair. Upon the chair were overcoats and
caps which he was able to identify as the property of
Penrod Schofield and Samuel Williams, but, as he
was not sure which pair of shoes belonged to Penrod
and which to Sam, he added both pairs to Maurice's
and carried them into the bathroom. Here he set
the plug in the tub, turned the faucets, and, after
looking about him and discovering large supplies of
all sorts in a wall cabinet, he tossed six cakes of green
soap into the tub. He let the soap remain in the
water to soften a little, and, returning to the dressing

room, whiled away the time in mixing and mismating
pairs of shoes along the walls, and also in tying
the strings of the mismated shoes together in hard
knots.

Throughout all this, his expression was grave and
intent; his bright eyes grew brighter, but he did not
smile. Carlie Chitten was a singular boy, though
not unique: he was an "only child," lived at a hotel,
and found life there favourable to the development
of certain peculiarities in his nature. He played a
lone hand, and with what precocious diplomacy he
played that curious hand was attested by the fact
that Carlie was brilliantly esteemed by parents and
guardians in general.

It must be said for Carlie that, in one way, his
nature was liberal. For instance, having come upstairs to prepare a vengenace upon Sam and Maurice
in return for their slurs upon his dancing, he did not
confine his efforts to the belongings of those two
alone. He provided every boy in the house with
something to think about later, when shoes should be
resumed; and he was far from stopping at that.
Casting about him for some material that he desired,
he opened a door of the dressing-room and found
himself confronting the apartment of Miss Lowe.

pon a desk he beheld the bottle of mucilage he anted, and, having taken possession of it, he alwed his eye the privilege of a rapid glance into a ressing table drawer, accidentally left open.

He returned to the dressing room, five seconds ter, carrying not only the mucilage but a "switch" orn by Miss Lowe when her hair was dressed in a shion different from that which she had favoured r the party. This "switch" he placed in the pocket a juvenile overcoat unknown to him, and then he ok the mucilage into the bathroom. There he scued from the water the six cakes of soap, placed ne in each of the six shoes, pounding it down securely to the toe of the shoe with the handle of a back rush. After that, Carlie poured mucilage into all x shoes impartially until the bottle was empty, en took them back to their former positions in the ressing room. Finally, with careful forethought, e placed his own shoes in the pockets of his overcoat, nd left the overcoat and his cap upon a chair near e outer door of the room. Then he went quietly ownstairs, having been absent from the festivities little less than twelve minutes. He had been nergetic—only a boy could have accomplished so uch in so short a time. In fact, Carlie had been so busy that his forgetting to turn off the faucets in the bathroom is not at all surprising.

No one had noticed his absence. That infectious pastime, "Gotcher bumpus," had broken out again, and the general dancing, which had been resumed upon the conclusion of "Les Papillons," was once more becoming demoralized. Despairingly the aunts Rennsdale and Miss Lowe brought forth from the rear of the house a couple of waiters and commanded them to arrest the ringleaders, whereupon hilarious terror spread among the outlaw band. Shouting tauntingly at their pursuers, they fled—and bellowing, trampling flight swept through every quarter of the house.

Refreshments quelled this outbreak for a time. The orchestra played a march; Carlie Chitten and Georgie Bassett, with Amy Rennsdale and Marjorie, formed the head of a procession, while all the boys who had retained their sense of decorum immediately sought partners and fell in behind. The outlaws, succumbing to ice cream hunger, followed suit, one after the other, until all of the girls were provided with escorts. Then, to the moral strains of "The Stars and Stripes Forever," the children paraded out to the dining-room. Two and two they marched, except at the extreme tail end of the line, where, since there were three more boys than girls at the party, the three left-over boys were placed. These three were also the last three outlaws to succumb and return to civilization from outlying portions of the house after the pursuit by waiters. They were Messieurs Maurice Levy, Samuel Williams, and Penrod Schofield.

They took their chairs in the capacious dining room quietly enough, though their expressions were eloquent of bravado, and they jostled one another and their neighbours intentionally, even in the act of sitting. However, it was not long before delectable foods engaged their whole attention and Miss Amy Rennsdale's party relapsed into etiquette for the following twenty minutes. The refection concluded with the mild explosion of paper "crackers," which erupted bright-coloured, fantastic headgear, and during the snapping of the "crackers," Penrod heard the voice of Marjorie calling from somewhere behind him, "Carlie and Amy, will you change chairs with Georgie Bassett and me—just for fun?" The chairs had been placed in rows, back to back, and Penrod would not even turn his head to see if Master Chitten and Miss Rennsdale accepted Marjorie's proposal, though they were directly behind him and Sam, but he grew red and breathed hard. A moment later, the liberty-cap which he had set upon his head was softly removed, and a little crown of silver paper put in its place.

"*Penrod ?*"

The whisper was close to his ear, and a gentle breath cooled the back of his neck.

CHAPTER XXIV

THE HEART OF MARJORIE JONES

"WELL, what you want?" Penrod asked, brusquely.

Marjorie's wonderful eyes were dark and mysterious, like still water at twilight.

"What makes you behave so *awful?*" she whispered.

"I don't either! I guess I got a right to do the way I want to, haven't I?"

"Well, anyway," said Marjorie, "you ought to quit bumping into people so it hurts."

"Poh! It wouldn't hurt a fly!"

"Yes, it did. It hurt when you bumped Maurice and me that time."

"It didn't either. *Where'd* it hurt you? Let's see if it——"

"Well, I can't show you, but it did. Penrod, are you going to keep on?"

Penrod's heart had melted within him, but his reply was pompous and cold. "I will if I feel like

345

it, and I won't if I feel like it. You wait and see."

But Marjorie jumped up and ran around to him abandoning her escort. All the children were leaving their chairs and moving toward the dancing-rooms; the orchestra was playing dance-music again.

"Come on, Penrod!" Marjorie cried. "Let's go dance this together. Come on!"

With seeming reluctance, he suffered her to lead him away. "Well, I'll go with you, but I won't dance," he said. "I wouldn't dance with the President of the United States!"

"Why, Penrod?"

"Well—because—well, I won't do it!"

"All right. I don't care. I guess I've danced plenty, anyhow. Let's go in here." She led him into a room too small for dancing, used ordinarily by Miss Amy Rennsdale's papa as his study, and now vacant. For a while there was silence, but finally Marjorie pointed to the window and said shyly:

"Look, Penrod, it's getting dark. The party'll be over pretty soon, and you've never danced one single time!"

"Well, I guess I know that, don't I?"

He was unable to cast aside his outward truculence, though it was but a relic. However, his voice was gentler, and Marjorie seemed satisfied. From the other rooms came the swinging music, shouts of "Gotcher bumpus!" sounds of stumbling, of scrambling, of running, of muffled concussions, and squeals of dismay. Penrod's followers were renewing the wild work, even in the absence of their chief.

"Penrod Schofield, you bad boy," said Marjorie, "you started every bit of that! You ought to be ashamed of yourself."

"*I* didn't do anything," he said—and he believed it. "Pick on me for everything!"

"Well, they wouldn't if you didn't do so much," said Marjorie.

"They would, too."

"They wouldn't, either. Who would?"

"That Miss Lowe," he specified bitterly. "Yes, and Baby Rennsdale's aunts. If the house'd burn down, I bet they'd say Penrod Schofield did it! Anybody does anything at *all*, they say, 'Penrod Schofield, shame on you!' When you and Carlie were dan——"

"Penrod, I just hate that little Carlie Chitten.

P'fesser Bartet made me learn that dance with him, but I just hate him."

Penrod was now almost completely mollified; nevertheless, he continued to set forth his grievance. "Well, they all turned around to me and they said, 'Why, Penrod Schofield, shame on you!' And I hadn't done a single thing! I was just standin' there. They got to blame *me*, though!"

Marjorie laughed airily. "Well, if you aren't the foolishest——"

"They would, too," he asserted, with renewed bitterness. "If the house was to fall down, you'd see! They'd all say——"

Marjorie interrupted him. She put her hand on the top of her head, looking a little startled.

"What's that?" she said.

"What's what?"

"Like rain!" Marjorie cried. "Like it was raining in here! A drop fell on my——"

"Why, it couldn't——" he began. But at this instant a drop fell upon his head, too, and, looking up, they beheld a great oozing splotch upon the ceiling. Drops were gathering upon it and falling; the tinted plaster was cracking, and a little stream began to patter down and splash upon the floor.

Then there came a resounding thump upstairs, just above them, and fragments of wet plaster fell.

"The roof must be leaking," said Marjorie, beginning to be alarmed.

"Couldn't be the roof," said Penrod. "Besides there ain't any rain outdoors."

As he spoke, a second slender stream of water began to patter upon the floor of the hall outside the door.

"Good gracious!" Marjorie cried, while the ceiling above them shook as with earthquake—or as with boys in numbers jumping, and a great uproar burst forth overhead.

"I believe the house *is* falling down, Penrod!" she quavered.

"Well, they'll blame *me* for it!" he said. "Anyways, we better get out o' here. I guess sumpthing must be the matter."

His guess was accurate, so far as it went. The dance-music had swung into "Home Sweet Home" some time before, the children were preparing to leave, and Master Chitten had been the first boy to ascend to the gentlemen's dressing-room for his cap, overcoat, and shoes, his motive being to avoid by departure any difficulty in case his earlier activities should cause him to be suspected by the other boys. But in the doorway he halted, aghast.

The lights had not been turned on, but even the dim windows showed that the polished floor gave back reflections no floor-polish had ever equalled. It was a gently steaming lake, from an eighth to a quarter of an inch deep. And Carlie realized that he had forgotten to turn off the faucets in the bathroom.

For a moment, his *savoir faire* deserted him, and he was filled with ordinary, human-boy panic. Then, at a sound of voices behind him, he lost his head and rushed into the bathroom. It was dark, but certain sensations and the splashing of his pumps warned him that the water was deeper in there. The next instant the lights were switched on in both bathroom and dressing-room, and Carlie beheld Sam Williams in the doorway of the former.

"Oh, look, Maurice!" Sam shouted, in frantic excitement. "Somebody's let the tub run over, and it's about ten feet deep! Carlie Chitten's sloshin' around in here. Let's hold the door on him and keep him in!"

Carlie rushed to prevent the execution of this project, but he slipped and went swishing full length

along the floor, creating a little surf before him as
he slid, to the demoniac happiness of Sam and Maurice. They closed the door, however, and, as other
boys rushed, shouting and splashing, into the flooded
dressing-room, Carlie began to hammer upon the
panels. Then the owners of shoes, striving to rescue them from the increasing waters, made discov-
eries.

The most dangerous time to give a large children's
party is when there has not been one for a long
period. The Rennsdale party had that misfortune,
and its climax was the complete and convulsive
madness of the gentlemen's dressing-room during
those final moments supposed to be given to quiet
preparations, on the part of guests, for departure.

In the upper hall and upon the stairway, panic-
stricken little girls listened, wild-eyed, to the uproar
that went on, while waiters and maid servants rushed
with pails and towels into what was essentially the
worst ward in Bedlam. Boys who had behaved
properly all afternoon now gave way and joined the
confraternity of lunatics. The floors of the house
shook to tramplings, rushes, wrestlings, falls, and
collisions. The walls resounded to chorused bel-

lowings and roars. There were pipings of pain and
pipings of joy; there was whistling to pierce the
drums of ears; there were hootings and howlings and
bleatings and screechings, while over all bleated the
heathen battle-cry incessantly: *"Gotcher bumpus !*
Gotcher bumpus !" For the boys had been inspired
by the unusual water to transform Penrod's game of
"Gotcher bumpus" into an aquatic sport, and to
induce one another, by means of superior force,
dexterity, or stratagems, either to sit or to lie at full
length in the flood, after the example of Carlie
Chitten.

One of the aunts Rennsdale had taken what charge
she could of the deafened and distracted maids and
waiters who were working to stem the tide, while
the other of the aunts Rennsdale stood with her niece
and Miss Lowe at the foot of the stairs, trying to
say good-night reassuringly to those of the terrified
little girls who were able to tear themselves away.
This latter aunt Rennsdale marked a dripping figure
which came unobtrusively, and yet in a self-contained
and gentlemanly manner, down the stairs.

"Carlie Chitten!" she cried. "You poor dear
child, you're soaking! To think those outrageous
little fiends wouldn't even spare *you !*" As she

spoke, another departing male guest came from behind Carlie and placed in her hand a snakelike
article—a thing which Miss Lowe seized and concealed with one sweeping gesture.

"It's some false hair somebody must of put in
my overcoat pocket," said Roderick Magsworth
Bitts. "Well, g'-night. Thank you for a very nice
time."

"Good-night, Miss Rennsdale," said Master Chitten demurely. "Thank you for a——"

But Miss Rennsdale detained him.

"Carlie," she said earnestly, "you're a dear boy,
and I know you'll tell me something. It was all
Penrod Schofield, wasn't it?"

"You mean he left the——"

"I mean," she said, in a low tone, not altogether
devoid of ferocity, "I mean it was Penrod who left
the faucets running, and Penrod who tied the boys'
shoes together, and filled some of them with soap
and mucilage, and put Miss Lowe's hair in Roddy
Bitts's overcoat. No; look me in the eye, Carlie!
They were all shouting that silly thing he started.
Didn't he do it?"

Carlie cast down thoughtful eyes. "I wouldn't
like to tell, Miss Rennsdale," he said. "I guess I

better be going or I'll catch cold. Thank you for a
very nice time." ·

"There!" said Miss Rennsdale vehemently, as
Carlie went on his way. "What did I tell you?
Carlie Chitten's too manly to say it, but I just *know*
it was that terrible Penrod Schofield."

Behind her, a low voice, unheard by all except the
person to whom it spoke, repeated a part of this
speech: "What did I tell you?"

This voice belonged to one Penrod Schofield.

Penrod and Marjorie had descended by another
stairway, and he now considered it wiser to pass to
the rear of the little party at the foot of the stairs.
As he was still in his pumps, his choked shoes occupy-
ing his overcoat pockets, he experienced no difficulty
in reaching the front door, and getting out of it
unobserved, although the noise upstairs was greatly
abated. Marjorie, however, made her courtesies
and farewells in a creditable manner.

"There!" said Penrod again, when she rejoined
him in the darkness outside. "What did I tell you?
Didn't I say I'd get the blame of it, no matter if the
house went and fell down? I s'pose they think I
put mucilage and soap in my own shoes."

Marjorie delayed at the gate until some eagerly

talking little girls had passed out. The name "Penrod Schofield" was thick and scandalous among them.

"Well," said Marjorie, "*I* wouldn't care, Penrod. 'Course, about soap and mucilage in *your* shoes, anybody'd know some other boy must of put 'em there to get even for what you put in his."

Penrod gasped.

"But I *didn't!*" he cried. "I didn't do *anything!* That ole Miss Rennsdale can say what she wants to, I didn't do a——"

"Well, anyway, Penrod," said Marjorie, softly, "they can't ever *prove* it was you."

He felt himself suffocating in a coil against which no struggle availed.

"But I never *did* it!" he wailed, helplessly. "I never did anything at all!"

She leaned toward him a little, and the lights from her waiting carriage illumined her dimly, but enough for him to see that her look was fond and proud, yet almost awed.

"Anyway, Penrod," she whispered, "*I* don't believe there's any other boy in the whole world could of done *half* as much!"

And with that she left him, and ran out to the carriage.

But Penrod remained by the gate to wait for Sam, and the burden of his sorrows was beginning to lift. In fact, he felt a great deal better, in spite of his having just discovered why Marjorie loved him.

THE END

THE COUNTRY LIFE PRESS, GARDEN CITY, NEW YORK

CPSIA information can be obtained
at www.ICGtesting.com
Printed in the USA
BVHW040320040720
582951BV00011B/181